Sewlicious

35 WAYS TO A HANDMADE WORLD

Kate Haxell

CICO BOOKS

LONDON NEW YORK

ABOUT THE AUTHOR
Kate Haxell is an experienced craft editor and author. She has written a wide range of craft and design books, including *Super-cute Pincushions*, *Vintage Hearts & Flowers*, *Quick and Easy Handmade Storage*, *Quick and Easy Handmade Garden Furniture*, and *The Seed Bead Book*, all published by CICO Books. She lives in south London. Visit her website at www.katehaxell.co.uk.

For Scarlet, with thanks.

Published in 2014 by CICO Books
An imprint of Ryland Peters & Small
519 Broadway, 5th Floor,
New York NY 10012
20–21 Jockey's Fields,
London WC1R 4BW
www.rylandpeters.com

10 9 8 7 6 5 4 3 2 1

A CIP catalog record for this book is available from the Library of Congress and the British Library.

ISBN: 978-1-78249-085-2

Printed in China

Editor: Katie Hardwicke
Designer: Elizabeth Healey
Project step illustration: Michael Hill
Technique and template illustration:
Stephen Dew
Photographers: Joanna Henderson and Penny Wincer
Stylists: Sania Pell and Catherine Woram

Contents

 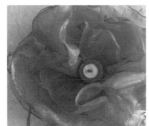  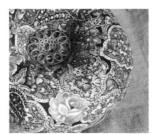 

Sewlicious

Introduction

"SEWLICIOUS" is a multi-talented kind of word: it's telling you that you can choose fabrics and trims that make you positively twinkle with pleasure, and use simple stitching to turn them into something you'll love to use / see / wear every day. It's reminding you that just because something is perfectly practical, it doesn't have to be ugly; that just because something is quick and easy to make, it doesn't have to be clunky; and that just because something is utterly frivolous, it doesn't have to be throwaway. "Sewlicious" is delicious sewing.

All that, in just one word…
Just one word, but 35 luscious fabric makes…

…which are all about you and your sewing, not me and mine; so you'll find thoughts and wriggles for making pieces your own. Some projects have bits you can miss out if time is tight or if you want a simpler option (look out for the **"MISS THIS BIT"** or the **"EXCELLENT NEWS"** tags in the steps), and others have design-tweak ideas and fabric musings that I hope will have you pondering all sorts of possibilities while wandering your fabric store.

And none of these projects need serious sewing skills; indeed, many of them are absolutely perfect for newly fledged sewists to experiment with. Only just learned to sew a straight(ish) line on your new-to-you sewing machine? Most of the Sewlicious designs will be more than happy with your skills and will give you fabulous results for not a lot of time and money. Never tried machine embroidery before? Dead Flowery (on page 23) is small, scribbly, and sweetly sinister: just perfect to mess with. Think patchwork is about über-vile bright fabrics and über-complicated twiddly squares? Trot on over to page 40 and go Groovalicious with a wonky-at-heart quilt that's sew simple.

So jump in, feet first please! Pick something to make for you, your home, your tent, your dog, your bestest friend, your favorite festival, your new sewcalist obsession…buy, recycle, raid some bits of fabric and trimming loveliness…arm yourself with scissors, needle, thread, sewing machine…follow the clear-but-gorgeous illustrations and hand-holding step-by-step instructions…and MAKE something! You're going to love doing it, and love what you've done.

Kate

chapter 1

At home
I HAVE...

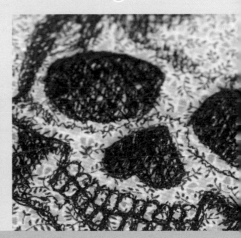

Rosy
PILLOWCASES

The matchy-matchy thing of bed linen sets doesn't appeal? It really is über-simple and seriously speedy to make your own pillowcases, and they can be as colorful and as multi-patterned as your eyes can cope with first thing in the morning. Make versions using fabrics leftover from either of the quilts (see Geektastic Quilt, page 18, and Groovalicious Patchwork, page 40) for a bedroom that's bursting with color and pattern, but is also harmonious.

YOU'RE GOING TO NEED...
- **Fabrics**: see How Much Fabric?, below
- Ruler
- Rotary cutter and cutting mat, or fabric scissors
- Pins
- Iron and ironing board
- Sewing threads to match fabrics
- Sewing machine

HOW MUCH FABRIC?
Measure the width and length of a pillowcase that fits your pillow: mine is 17¾in (45cm) wide by 27¼in (69cm) long. Multiply the length by 2, so 54½in (138cm), and add 6¾in (17cm) for a flap and 3in (8cm) for a hem, so 64¼in (163cm) in total. To the width, just add 1¼in (3cm) for seam allowances, so 19in (48cm). So, 19 x 64¼in (48 x 163cm) is the size I needed to piece together.

1 Cut pieces of fabrics and sew them together, taking ⅝-in (1.5-cm) seam allowances, to make a finished piece the right size. Zigzag the seam allowances together (for durability: these pillowcases are going to get used, and so washed, a lot), and press them to one side.

2 Decide which end of the piece will be the internal flap that holds the pillow in. At that end, press under a double ⅜in (1cm) hem. At the other end, press a double 1½in (4cm) hem. Sew the hems close to the edges.

3 Some of the folding in the next couple of steps might seem counter-intuitive, but trust me... Lay the piece face down and fold back 6in (15cm) for the flap at the end with the smaller hem. Press the fold.

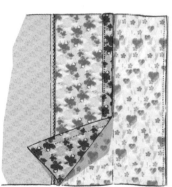

4 | Turn the whole piece face up and open out the flap. Fold up the other end so that the hem lies against the pressed fold.

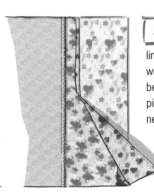

5 | Fold the flap over the hem up to the pressed line: the fold will be "facing the wrong way" at this stage, but it'll be the right way on the finished pillowcase, and I always get a neater result doing it like this.

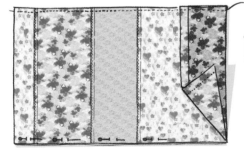

6 | Pin and then sew the side seams, reversing at each end to secure the stitches. Then zigzag stitch the seam allowances. Turn the pillowcase right side out, and the flap will neatly enclose the seams. Now make your bed and lie in it!

YOU'RE GOING TO NEED...

- Templates on page 143
- Paper for templates
- Paper scissors and fabric scissors
- Thick, sharp sewing needle
- 8 x 12in (20 x 30cm) of medium-weight cream fabric, for the head
- 8 x 6in (20 x 15cm) of medium-weight fusible interfacing
- Iron and ironing board
- Fading fabric marker
- 6in (15cm) embroidery hoop
- Embroidery floss in pale green, darker green, mid-brown, dark brown, cream, mid-pink, darker pink
- Embroidery needle
- Toile de Jouy fabric measuring 18 x 16in (45 x 40cm), though it's best to have a bit extra so that you can place the pattern to best effect on the body
- Sewing threads to match fabrics
- Sewing machine
- 6¼ x 6¼in (16 x 16cm) of wool felt for the boots
- Hand-sewing needle
- Toy stuffing
- 1¼ x 10in (3 x 25cm) strip of card
- Cotton perlé embroidery floss, for the bootlaces
- Yarn for hair: I used two shades of mid-brown 4-ply yarn and a small amount of pink 4-ply
- Knitting needles (if you want curly hair)
- Two pieces of medium-weight fabric measuring 4½ x 4in (11.5 x 10cm), for the bodice
- One piece of lightweight fabric measuring 39 x 7½in (100 x 19cm), for the skirt
- Two pieces of net measuring 39 x 5in (100 x 13cm), for the petticoat
- 12in (30cm) of lace
- Scrap of ribbon, beads, and buttons for jewelry

Tattooed
LADY

In the 1970s, my rag doll, Araminta Prodnose, had a groovy patterned tunic and long, stripy trousers, tumbling hair, wide eyes, and a very long nose. This new doll, Araminta Tattoo, is made from Toile de Jouy fabric for instant cherub and rose tattoos, and is wearing a vintage ensemble of a Fifties dress and Seventies boots to go with her retro updo. If embroidery isn't your thing, you can give her appliqué features cut from felt—see Making Faces, page 14. This isn't a quick project, but true glamour does take time to achieve…

MAKING THE FACE

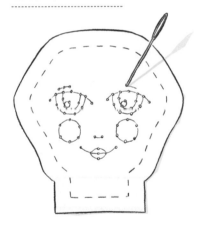

2   Iron the interfacing onto the wrong side of half of the fabric (it'll help stabilize the embroidery). Lay the template on the interfaced fabric and hold or pin it in place. Press the fabric marker over each pricked hole in the template to make a dot-to-dot drawing on the fabric.

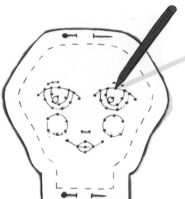

1   Enlarge the head template by 200 percent and cut it out around the solid line. Using a thick, sharp sewing needle, such as a chenille needle, prick holes along the lines of the features, spacing them about ¼in (6mm) apart, and making sure that there is a hole at the end of every line and where lines meet.

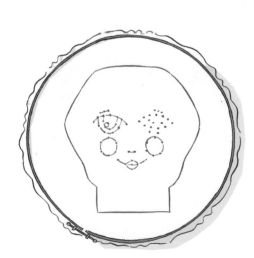

3   Lift the template off the fabric and join all the dots. Fit the face fabric into the embroidery hoop.

4 Embroider the face as follows (or see Making Faces, right, for alternative ideas).

Eyes: Outline the lower edge of the irises in split stitch (see page 135) with two strands of dark green floss, then the irises in satin stitch (see page 135)—with the stitches fanned around to follow the shape—in two strands of dark green and one of pale green held together. Outline the lower edge of the pupils and the edge of the highlights with split stitch in two strands of dark brown, then fill the pupils with vertical satin stitch in three strands of dark brown. The highlights are four French knots (see page 134) made with two strands of cream. Eyelids and eyebrows are stem and outline stitched (see page 136) in mid-brown.

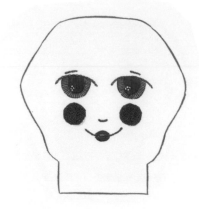

MAKING FACES
To make an appliqué face, cut out the eye sections, the cheeks, and the pout from the template. Use these as templates to cut colored felt pieces. Either sew these on to the head with tiny running stitches using matching sewing threads, or glue them on using fabric glue. The eyebrows, eyelids, and nose can either be embroidered in simple backstitch using floss, or drawn on using fabric pens or paints.

Cheeks: Starting on the outside edge, embroider concentric circles of chain stitch (see page 134) in one strand of dark pink and one of mid-pink held together.

Nose: Work a line of stem stitch in dark brown.

Lips: Outline the pout in split stitch with two strands of dark pink and then fill it in with vertical satin stitches using the same floss. Embroider the smile in backstitch (see page 133) in two strands of mid-pink.

MAKING THE BODY

5 Enlarge the body template by 200 percent and cut it out around the solid line, then cut out the middle of the template along the dotted line, the seam line. Use the template as a frame, laying it on the toile fabric and positioning a motif to best effect on the upper chest. Cut out two body pieces, cutting around the outside of the template. Cut two arms and two legs the same way. Remember that the seam will run down the back of the legs, and that the arms will need the toile motifs placing differently to make a left and a right arm.

6 Fold each leg piece in half, right sides together, and sew the long seam. Take ⅜-in (1-cm) seam allowances throughout, unless otherwise stated. Press the stitching only: don't press the legs flat. Turn right side out.

7 Enlarge the boot template by 200 percent and cut four boots from felt. Pair them up and sew the pairs together around the edges using blanket stitch (see page 133) and sewing thread, leaving the top edge open. Stuff the heels and toes as you go, then stuff the whole boot when the sewing is complete.

8 Slide the strip of card into a leg, then slip the pointed end of the leg into the top of a boot. Tuck about ⅜in (1cm) of leg into the top of the boot and pin it in place (the card will make it easier to pin, and sew, just one side of a leg at a time). Blanket stitch the leg in place around the top of the boot, then take out the card. Repeat with the other leg and boot.

9 Stuff about half the leg, not very firmly, then work a row of continuous running stitch (see page 135) across it. Stuff the rest of the leg and oversew the top edge closed.

10 Use cotton perlé floss and an embroidery needle to sew laces on each boot. Start at the top, leaving a long tail, and make three diagonal stitches down the front of the boot. Then work back up to the top, completing the cross stitches. Leave long tails of floss at the beginning and end of the stitching, then tie those into bows.

11 Fold each arm in half, right sides facing. Sew the curved shoulder seam, then sew around the rest of the arm, leaving the short straight edge open. Cut notches in the seam allowances around the curved sections, as shown, cutting to within about ⅛in (3mm) of the stitching. Trim all the seam allowances to ¼in (6mm). Turn the arms right side out and stuff them, then oversew the open end closed.

12 Cut out the embroidered head and cut a second, plain, head from the rest of the cream fabric. Right sides together, pin the embroidered head to the body front at the neck. Sew them together across the neck. Repeat with the plain head and the body back.

13 Place the arms on the body front, as shown, and baste them in position along the oversewn seams.

14 | Right sides together, lay the body back on top of the body front and pin the pieces together around the edges. Make sure the arms are well tucked in so that only the oversewn edges get caught in the stitching. Sew the bodies together, leaving the bottom edge open. Turn right side out and stuff firmly, making sure the neck is particularly firmly stuffed so it doesn't droop.

15 | Turn under ⅜in (1cm) at the open edge on the bottom of the body. Tuck the tops of the legs into the body, making sure the boots point forward, and pin them in place. Machine- or hand-sew right across the pinned seam to attach the legs.

16 | To make curly hair, you need knitted yarn. If you don't knit, then either get a friend to help (tell them it's just a bit of very simple garter stitch), or make straight hair from un-knitted yarn. Cast on 30 sts and knit 60 rows using two toning yarns held together. Steam the knitting with an iron, holding it just above the surface, then let dry. Cut along the row ends on one edge and unravel the strands of yarn. Sew strands of yarn to the head along the parting to make a hairdo, see Doing an Updo, right.

DOING AN UPDO
You can make any sort of hairdo you want. To make Araminta's updo, I started by sewing on long strands draped across the top of her head and stitched down along a side parting. I sewed on about ten strands, then added the pink strand, then ten more brown strands, running across onto the back of her head. I looped the strands around to the back, curled them, and stitched them down on the back of her head, building up the updo. I didn't pull the strands too taut, left a few bits looser still, and left some of the ends as messy tufts on the very top of the do.

MAKING THE DRESS

17 | Press under a ⅜in (1cm) hem on both short sides and one long side of both bodice pieces. Miter the corners neatly.

18 | Sew a piece of lace across each folded long edge. Sew through all layers, making the stitches tiny so they are invisible on the lace. Fitting the bodice will depend a bit on the positions of your doll's tattoos, so pin the front bodice (either piece will do) to the doll's front and mark where the side seams will come to under her arms.

16 **AT HOME I HAVE...**

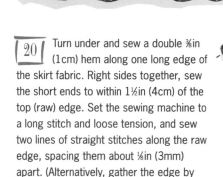

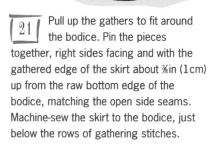

19 Place the two bodice pieces right sides together, open out the hems at one side, and sew one side seam up to the marked point. Leave the other seam open. Wrap the bodice around the doll, pin it in place, then pin pieces of lace in position as shoulder straps. Take the bodice off and sew the straps in place.

20 Turn under and sew a double ⅜in (1cm) hem along one long edge of the skirt fabric. Right sides together, sew the short ends to within 1½in (4cm) of the top (raw) edge. Set the sewing machine to a long stitch and loose tension, and sew two lines of straight stitches along the raw edge, spacing them about ⅛in (3mm) apart. (Alternatively, gather the edge by hand using running stitches.)

21 Pull up the gathers to fit around the bodice. Pin the pieces together, right sides facing and with the gathered edge of the skirt about ⅜in (1cm) up from the raw bottom edge of the bodice, matching the open side seams. Machine-sew the skirt to the bodice, just below the rows of gathering stitches.

22 Sew a line of running stitches along one long edge of the petticoat net. Pull up the gathers to fit around the raw edge of the bodice. With the wrong side of the gathered edge against the right side of the bodice, machine-sew the petticoat to the bottom of the bodice using a small zigzag stitch, matching the open edge to the open side of the dress.

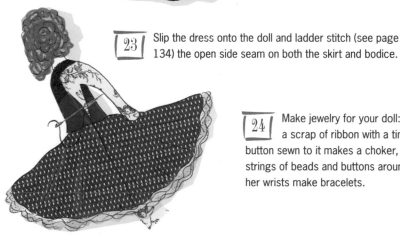

23 Slip the dress onto the doll and ladder stitch (see page 134) the open side seam on both the skirt and bodice.

24 Make jewelry for your doll: a scrap of ribbon with a tiny button sewn to it makes a choker, and strings of beads and buttons around her wrists make bracelets.

Geektastic QUILT

SEAM ALLOWANCES

Quilts usually have ¼-in (6-mm) seam allowances, but as there are only a few pieces in this quilt, the larger seam allowance won't make the patchwork too lumpy, and it is easier to sew. If you prefer the narrower seam allowance, you can reduce the size of each square by ¼in (6mm) all around.

If "Fibonacci sequence" means nothing to you, then take a quick wander on the Web to marvel at its curiously gorgeous properties. Beloved of geeks the world over, this mathematical pattern also makes for an easy-to-put-together quilt. I've chosen riotous prints and dialled down the craziness by using only two main color palettes but a more minimal version in shades of slate, taupe, lavender, and gray with the spots in tones of cream would be elegantly delicious. The finished size is 66¾ x 44in (171 x 112cm), but changing the scale of all the squares will make a larger or smaller version.

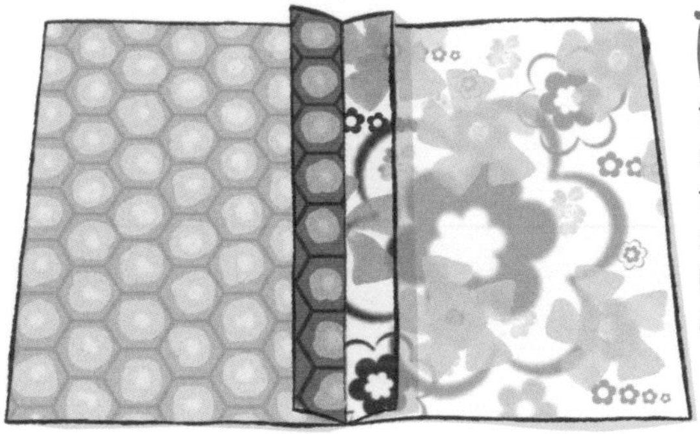

1 Start by piecing together the two smallest squares, taking a ⅜-in (1-cm) seam allowance. Press the seam allowances open.

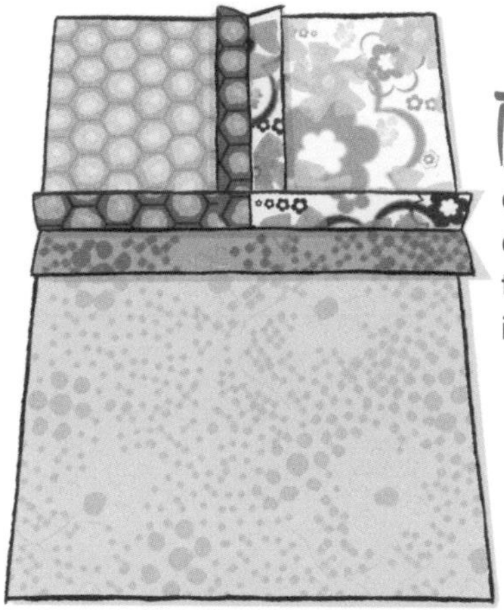

2 Following the layout diagram, piece each square to the previous ones in turn.

YOU'RE GOING TO NEED...

- Quilt layout diagram on page 139
- Fabrics: see How Much Fabric?, right
- Ruler
- Rotary cutter and cutting mat, or fabric scissors
- Pins
- Iron and ironing board
- Sewing threads to match fabrics
- Sewing machine with free-motion embroidery function (if you want to do the embroidery on the machine...)
- Length of yarn or thin twine (string)
- Water-soluble fabric marker
- Compasses
- Fusible webbing
- Batting measuring 71¼ x 48in (181 x 122cm): I used 100 percent cotton batting
- Quilter's safety pins (optional)

HOW MUCH FABRIC?

You absolutely must work in either imperial or metric as the measurements are worked out specifically in both, not converted from one to the other.

For the squares: two squares measuring 2½in (6.5cm), one square of each measuring 4¼in (11cm), 6in (15.5cm), 9½in (24.5cm), 14¾in (38cm), 23½in (60.5cm), and 37½in (96.5cm).

For the circles: scraps of fabrics to cut six ⅜in (1cm) diameter circles, two ¾in (2cm), two 1⅛in (3cm), three 1½in (4cm), two 1⅞in (5cm), three 2¼in (6cm), three 2⅝in (7cm), two 3in (8cm), and one of each of 3⅜in (9cm), 3¾in (10cm), 4⅛in (11cm), and 4½in (12cm) in diameter.

For the border: two strips measuring 37½ x 4in (96.5 x 10cm) and two measuring 67¼ x 4in (171 x 10cm)

For the quilt backing: a piece of fabric measuring 71¼ x 48in (181 x 122cm), or several pieces joined to make a backing this size

For the binding: a strip measuring 6½yd (6m) long by 3¾in (9.5cm) wide: this is 20in (50cm) of 55-in (140-cm) wide fabric, or 23½in (60cm) of 44-in (112-cm) wide fabric, including extra for joining strips (see Step 12).

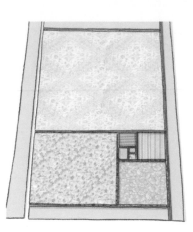

3 When all the squares are joined, add the borders in the same way. Sew the shorter border strips to the top and bottom of the quilt, then sew the longer ones to the sides.

4 Mark out the spiral on the quilt top, a square at a time. (Geektastic fact: this Fibonacci spiral is close to, often mistaken for, but not identical to a golden spiral, which is the product of the golden section.) You can do this by eye, following the layout diagram on page 139 (we don't need to be mathematically precise here), or you can mark each square in turn, as shown. Tie one end of a length of yarn to the fabric marker and use it as a compass, with the other point being a pin holding the yarn in place, to draw an arc across each square.

5 Draw out the various circles needed onto the paper backing of fusible webbing. Iron the pieces of webbing onto the backs of scraps of fabrics, making sure you've got a good variety of patterns, then cut out the circles.

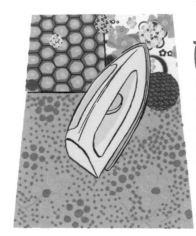

6 Arrange the circles on the spiral, spacing them by eye and using the photograph on page 22 and the layout diagram as guides. Remove the paper backing and pin each one in place. Dampen the fabric to remove the spiral line before ironing the circles in position: this is important as pen marks may become permanent when you iron them (says the voice of bitter experience).

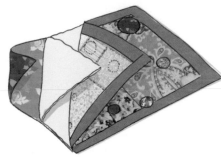

7 You can sew the circles on either using free-motion machine embroidery, which is what I did, or using hand stitches. The effect will be quite different, but both are good looks. I just "scribbled" around the edge of each circle with straight stitch, not worrying too much about making the lines very tidy (or very circular). If you are going to hand stitch, then that is best done in Step 11, so you can quilt at the same time. You could consider blanket stitch (see page 133) or chain stitch (see page 134), or simple running stitch (see page 135).

8 To make the quilt sandwich it's best to work on the floor, or on a stripped double bed. First lay the backing out right side down, making sure that it is flat and smooth; if you are working on the floor then use masking tape at intervals along the edges to hold the fabric flat, and if you are on a bed, then use curved quilter's safety pins to hold it in position. Lay the batting flat on top of the backing, then center the quilt top on the stack, making sure it is squared-up and smooth.

10 I stitched-in-the-ditch with the sewing machine along each seamline, but you could work lines of small running stitches by hand if you prefer that style of quilting. Start with the smallest squares, and work outward until you have sewn along the inner edges of the border strips. I quilted around each circle by "scribbling" a few more free-motion lines, but you could hand embroider at this stage (see Step 7). One thing I loved about using the free-motion technique is that it draws the fabric in a bit, making the circles slightly puffy.

9 Pin the layers together. I am a huge fan of curved safety pins, which allow you to pin without wrinkling up the fabric, and handle the pinned quilt without lacerating yourself. The safety pins do take the tiniest bit longer to remove as you sew than straight pins do, but a few seconds delay is worth not losing blood for, IMO. Pin along the seamlines and close to the edge of each larger circle.

11 When you have finished all the quilting, zigzag right around the edges of the quilt top, then trim off any excess batting and backing. Take out all the safety pins.

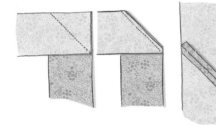

12 Cut 3¾in (9.5cm) strips of binding. To join them at an angle (so making the finished binding less lumpy at these joins), lay two pieces right sides together at a right angle, as shown. Sew from corner to corner, then trim the seam allowance to ⅜in (1cm). Open the strip out flat and press the seam allowances open.

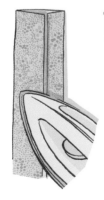

13 Measure in 1½in (4cm) from one edge and fold and press the fabric at that line. Do this right along the length. Then open out and fold the raw edges in to almost, but not quite, meet on the pressed line, and press again. Fold the binding along the original pressed line, then press for a final time.

14 Open out the narrower folded edge of the binding. Starting about 6in (15cm) from a corner, pin the binding to one edge of the quilt, matching the raw edge of the binding to the edge of the quilt (you'll probably only need to pin the first little bit, then you can just sew and match the edges as you go). Starting 1in (2.5cm) from the beginning of the binding, sew the binding in place along the visible pressed line, stopping ¾in (2cm) before you reach the corner of the quilt. Fasten off the threads.

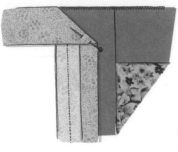

15 Fold the binding over at 45 degrees, as shown, and pin the inner edge of the fold in place. For a really neat miter, the fold should run directly to the corner of the quilt.

16 Fold the binding back on itself so that the raw edge is aligned with the next edge of the quilt to be bound: the fold should be square against the first edge, as shown. Starting right at the fold, and reversing to secure the stitching, sew along the pressed line of the binding. Repeat the process at each corner of the quilt.

17 At the last corner, fold the binding at an angle as usual. At the start of the binding, open out the other folded edge and press the whole loose end over at an angle, as shown. Lay the free end over this fold and trim off any excess. Sew the binding in place, then fold the opened-out upper section over the short end.

18 Fold the binding over to the back of the quilt. At the corners, miter it neatly; it should happily cooperate with this.

19 On the right side, stitch-in-the-ditch, either by machine or with hand running stitches, along the binding seamline. Sew slowly, smoothing the back layer of the binding flat as you go so that it is all caught into the stitching. Pivot neatly at the corners.

Dead

FLOWERY

YOU'RE GOING TO NEED...

- 12-in (30-cm) square of pale, floral, medium-weight fabric: I used needlecord
- 6-in (15-cm) diameter circle of lightweight fusible interfacing
- Skull template on page 140
- Fading fabric marker
- 8in (20cm) (for working) and 6in (15cm) (for framing) embroidery hoops
- Fabric scissors
- Iron and ironing board
- Pins
- Black sewing thread
- Black six-strand embroidery floss
- Strong sewing thread
- Sewing machine with free-motion embroidery foot
- Hand-sewing and embroidery needles
- Black paint or permanent marker pen
- 6-in (15-cm) square of felt
- Sewing thread to match felt
- Ribbon for hanging

Cute and gothic? Must be chibi goth… I've worked this embroidery in both free-motion machine stitching and hand stitching, but you could use just one technique if that's the one you love best. And if you've never tried machine embroidery before, this is a good, scribbly, small project to experiment with. I've framed my skull in an embroidery hoop, but you can put yours into a picture frame if you prefer.

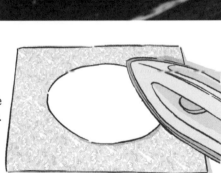

1   Iron the circle of fusible webbing onto the back of the fabric, positioning it centrally.

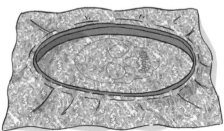

2   Follow Steps 1–3 of Tattooed Lady (see page 13) to transfer the template onto the interfaced area of the fabric and fix it into the larger embroidery hoop. Fix the fabric into the hoop with the inner ring on top, so that the fabric is flat across the bottom of the hoop for machine embroidery.

3 Set up the machine for free-motion embroidery by lowering the feed dogs, fitting the embroidery foot, and setting the stitch length to zero; see Machine Embroidery, right, for some tips on this technique if you've never done it before. Start by outlining the skull and main features with a couple of lines of stitching. Then build up the detail a little at a time. Don't try and follow the drawn lines faithfully; be a bit scribbly to give your skull some character of its own.

MACHINE EMBROIDERY

If you've never done this before, it would be best to practice a bit on scrap fabric, just to get the feel of moving the fabric around under the needle. Because the feed dogs are lowered, they aren't feeding the fabric through under the needle, so you need to move the fabric yourself. It's usually best to do this in a hoop, as that keeps the fabric taut and you can hold the hoop to steer the fabric. You might need to fiddle with the tension setting on your machine to get it right for embroidery.

Don't be tempted to sew very slowly; it's actually easier to embroider with a bit of speed. You're aiming to move the fabric smoothly under the needle, drawing with the resulting stitches.

Machine embroidery is addictive: once you've got the hang of it you'll just want more…

4 Add more depth and detail with some hand stitches. I used two strands from six-strand embroidery floss and trellis stitch and chain stitch (see pages 136 and 134). Keep working into areas until you are happy with your embroidered skull.

5 Stain the outer ring of the 6in (15cm) hoop black, either by painting it or by coloring it with a permanent marker pen, which is what I did. You don't need to stain the inside of the outer ring, or any of the inner ring.

6 Lay the inner ring on the felt and draw around the inside of it. Cut out a circle of felt, cutting just inside the drawn ring. Set this circle aside.

7 Fix the embroidery tightly into the hoop, with the outer ring on top this time. Make sure the tightening screw is at the top. Cut the excess fabric into a circle, about 1½in (4cm) outside the hoop.

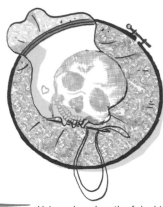

8 Using a long length of doubled strong sewing thread, work a line of gathering stitches around the edge of the fabric circle, on the back of the work.

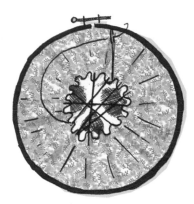

9 Pull the gathers up as tight as possible, then make stitches across the opening to pull it tight and flat.

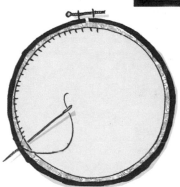

10 Center the circle of felt on the back of the embroidery, covering the gathered opening. Using matching sewing thread and blanket stitch, sew around the edges. Loop a piece of ribbon around the tightening screw to hang the hoop by. I added a few tiny paper flowers to the top as well, just for extra goth cuteness.

Let
SLEEPING DOGS LIE...

YOU'RE GOING TO NEED...

- Head, tail, ear, and leg templates on page 141
- Paper for templates
- Ruler and pencil
- Sticky tape
- Paper and fabric scissors
- Two pieces of fabric measuring 10in (25cm) by the length of your door/window plus ¾in (2cm) for the body, two pieces measuring 16 x 4in (40 x 10cm) for the ears (use a contrast fabric for the inner ear), and eight pieces measuring 6¾ x 4in (17 x 10cm) for the legs: I used needlecord for the body, outer ears, and legs, and quilting cotton for the inner ears
- Two large and two small buttons for eyes, and four large buttons to hold legs on
- Scraps of felt
- Fabric marker pen
- Pins
- Hand-sewing needle
- Sewing threads to match fabrics
- Sewing machine
- Iron and ironing board
- Small pom-pom: I cut one from a piece of furnishing trim
- Toy stuffing
- Very long sewing needle, such as a doll needle
- Strong sewing thread, such as buttonhole thread

If you live in an efficiently insulated house, just pretend it's drafty then you have an excuse for a fabulously retro doggie to snooze in front of your door or along your windowsill. Vincent (so called because he's orange) is completely adjustable in length to fit any door or window. And he does make an excellent child's toy (not for babies due to the buttons and pom-pom) if you really can't justify him as a draft excluder.

1 Enlarge all the templates by 200 percent. Decide on the length you want your finished dog to be and cut a strip of paper measuring that length by 4¾in (12cm). Tape the dog head and tail to the strip to make a complete template the right length. Cut out two bodies, four front legs, and four back legs (remembering to fold the fabric or flip the templates to get right-hand and left-hand pieces for each). Fold the ear fabrics in half and pin the straight edge of the template to the fold, then cut out a folded ear from each piece.

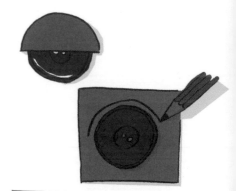

2 Make eyelids for your dog by laying the large eye buttons on the felt and drawing around part of them to make a semicircle, then cutting out the shapes, adding a small border to the circumference. I've made quite large eyelids, as Vincent is definitely a snoozy dog.

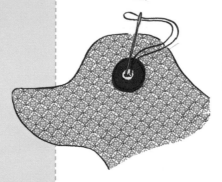

3 Sew the button eyes to the middle of the rounded part of the dog's head. Sew on a larger button topped by a smaller button: I've used a brown button topped by a pearl one for rather sleepy eyes, but you could use a colored button topped by a black one for bright eyes.

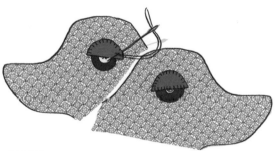

4 Pin an eyelid in position over each eye. Using doubled sewing thread to match the felt and starting at one end of the curve, blanket stitch (see page 133) the curve of the eyelid to the head. Then carry the stitching on across the straight edge of the eyelid and secure the thread on the back of the head.

5 Pin the two body pieces right sides together. Taking a ⅜-in (1-cm) seam allowance, machine-sew all around, leaving a small gap in the tummy for turning through. Clip notches into the seam allowances around all curved sections (see page 132), then turn the dog right side out and press the seam open.

6 Pair up the leg pieces, right sides together, to make two front and two back legs. Sew seams, leaving a small gap in one edge, and clip seam allowances as for the body (see Step 5), then turn right side out and press.

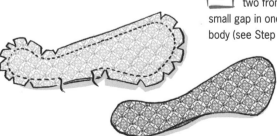

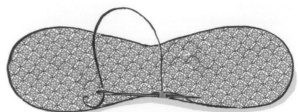

7 Open the inner and outer ear pieces out flat (they should each look like an elongated figure 8), and, right sides together, sew seams and clip seam allowances as for the body (see Step 5), leaving a gap near the middle. Turn right side out and press the ears flat, then ladder stitch (see page 134) the gap closed.

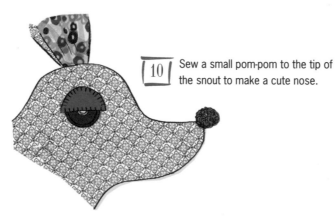

8 Lay the ears face down and make a pleat in the middle, as shown, so that the width of the middle is reduced to 1⅛in (3cm). Hand-sew the pleat in place with tiny stitches that aren't visible on the other side.

9 Sew the pleated middle of the ears to the seam on the top of the dog's head, again using small stitches into the pleat, but making sure they aren't visible on the outside of the ears.

10 Sew a small pom-pom to the tip of the snout to make a cute nose.

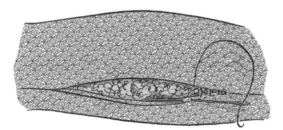

11 Stuff the body and legs with toy stuffing: stuff the head, neck, and tail very firmly, but fill the body of the dog more lightly. Stuff all the legs firmly. Ladder stitch all the gaps closed.

12 Thread the long needle with a long length of strong thread, double it, and knot the ends. To sew on the front legs, first make an anchoring stitch in one side of the chest at the spot marked by a star on the template. Then push the needle straight through the body so that it emerges on the other side in exactly the same spot (or close to it; your dog won't stand up so it doesn't matter if he's a bit wonky legwise).

13 Thread on a front leg, taking the needle through the leg at the starred spot on the template, then go through one hole in a button, back down through the other hole, then take the needle back through the body where it came through the first time. Thread on the other leg then a button, then take the needle through all the elements (button, leg, body, leg, button) several times. Finish and secure the thread on the opposite side of the body to the starting knot. Repeat the process to attach the back legs.

Bubble

AND STRIPE

YOU'RE GOING TO NEED...

- One piece of main fabric measuring 25 x 22¾in (63 x 57cm): I used cotton
- One piece of lining fabric measuring 19½ x 22¾in (49 x 57cm): I used curtain lining
- Fabric scissors
- Iron and ironing board
- Pins
- 47in (120cm) of piping cord
- Sewing threads to match fabrics
- Sewing machine with zipper foot
- Fading fabric marker
- Topstitch or quilting sewing thread
- Hand-sewing needle
- Small, sharp embroidery scissors
- Toy stuffing
- Knitting needle or chopstick
- Bolster form (pad) measuring 17¾in (45cm) long and 21¾in (54cm) circumference
- Two 5-in (13-cm) diameter circles of felt

I like to have layers of blankets and cushions in a mix of shapes and sizes on my sofa, just because I like the way they look together. This easy-to-make bolster has trapunto "bubbles" and piping, both simple enough to do, but both optional: see the **MISS THIS** bits in the steps (but do bear in mind that the piping helps give the gathered ends of the bolster their fab shape).

1 Lay the main fabric right side down. Measure down 2¾in (7cm) from each short end and press a fold right across (so the area of main fabric between the pressed folds measures 19½ x 22¾in/49 x 57cm, the same size as the lining fabric.) **MISS THIS** if you don't want to pipe the bolster, and cut the main fabric 1½in (4cm) shorter—so it's 23½ x 22¾in (59 x 57cm). Lay the piece of lining fabric right side down on the back of the main fabric, matching the raw edges and pressed folds of the main fabric—or centering it on the main fabric if you aren't piping.

2 Cut the piping cord in half. Lay out one length of cord close to a pressed fold, approximately ⅜in (1cm) below the edge of the lining, then fold the lining and main fabric tightly over the cord and pin along the fold, as shown. You might find it easier to baste along the fold at this stage to make sure that the piping cord is tightly encased by the fabric. Obviously **MISS THIS**, and the next step, if you aren't piping.

3 Fit a zipper foot to the sewing machine and sew along the pressed fold, encasing the piping. Repeat Steps 2–3 on the other pressed fold.

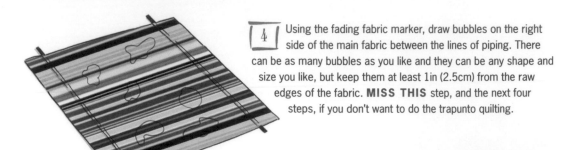

4 Using the fading fabric marker, draw bubbles on the right side of the main fabric between the lines of piping. There can be as many bubbles as you like and they can be any shape and size you like, but keep them at least 1in (2.5cm) from the raw edges of the fabric. **MISS THIS** step, and the next four steps, if you don't want to do the trapunto quilting.

5 Using doubled topstitch or quilting thread, work a line or tiny running stitches (see page 135) around each bubble, stitching through both layers of fabric. Start with a knot on the lining side, and finish with a few backstitches through the lining only. After this stage, make sure that the marker lines have vanished before moving on; you may find that dampening the fabric helps to remove them.

6 On the lining side, use small, sharp scissors to snip a slit in the lining fabric within each bubble outline. The cut should be at least ⅜in (1cm) in from the stitching at any point, and be very careful not to cut the main fabric.

7 Lightly stuff the bubble with toy stuffing. You can use a knitting needle or chopstick to push stuffing into the corners, but keep it soft rather than firmly packed in.

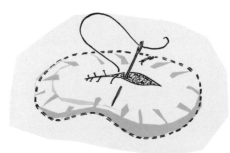

8 Sew up the slit using lacing stitch. To work this, slip the point of the needle into the slit and up through the fabric on one side, then do the same on the other side. Make stitches on alternate sides along the length of the slit, gently pulling the cut edges together as you go. Stuff and sew up every bubble.

9 Fold the fabric in half with right sides together to make a tube, matching the ends of the piping on either side. Baste the seam to make sure that the piping doesn't slip when you machine-sew. Taking a ⅝-in (1.5-cm) seam allowance, sew the seam, sewing straight over the ends of the piping at the top and bottom of the tube. Then turn under and press a ⅜-in (1-cm) hem around the raw ends.

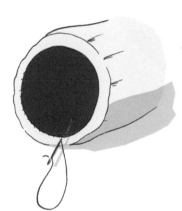

10 Center a circle of felt on each end of the bolster form (pad) and whip stitch (see page 133) it in position.

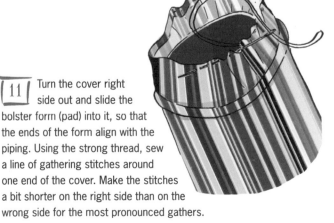

11 Turn the cover right side out and slide the bolster form (pad) into it, so that the ends of the form align with the piping. Using the strong thread, sew a line of gathering stitches around one end of the cover. Make the stitches a bit shorter on the right side than on the wrong side for the most pronounced gathers.

12 Pull on both ends of the thread to pull the gathers up as tightly as possible, then knot the threads very firmly. Thread the ends into a needle and take them down through a trough in the gathers to the back. Repeat Steps 11–12 on the other end of the cover.

Head

IN THE CLOUDS

- Templates on page 139
- Two pieces of fur fabric the size you want the cushion to be: I used a lamb fleece-type fur rather than a fluffy toy-type
- Pieces of patterned cotton fabrics for the raindrops and sunrays: I recycled bits from a shirt (the raindrops) and vintage skirt (the sunrays)
- Fading fabric marker
- Fabric scissors
- Iron and ironing board
- Pins
- Sewing threads to match fabrics
- Sewing machine
- Hand-sewing needle
- Basting thread: I always use ordinary sewing thread in a contrast color

Dream a day away (or just a stolen hour or so) on a fluffy cloud cushion. There are raindrops on one side to suit a pensive mood, and a burst of sunrays on the other for big, bright days. This cushion can be made almost any size: mine is a giant beanbag version, measuring about 1yd (1m) across and filled with polystyrene beads, but a smaller version filled with fiber stuffing would be very snuggly. There are templates for all the shapes, but I suggest you use them as a guide and draw the shapes out freehand: they really are very simple.

1 Lay one piece of fur fabric out flat and face down. Using the templates as a guide, draw a cloud onto the back of the fabric. Cut it out and pin it, right sides together, to the other piece of fur. Cut around the first piece to cut out the second. Separate the pieces.

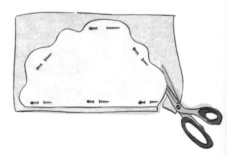

2 Using the templates, draw raindrop shapes onto the back of a piece of printed cotton fabric and cut them out. I have used three large drops, but you could make more and have a shower.

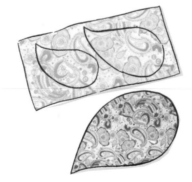

3 Pin and then baste the raindrops to the right side of one cloud, following the photograph for position, if you want. Keep the basting stitches about ⅜in (1cm) in from the edges of the drops.

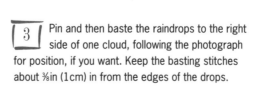

4 | Set the sewing machine to a narrow, tight zigzag or satin stitch. Position a raindrop under the needle so that the stitching will just overlap the edge, then stitch all around the drop to appliqué it to the cloud. Repeat to sew on all the drops. If you've not done machine appliqué before, see Appliqué Advice, below, for some tips. If you really hate the idea of machine appliqué, you can back the drops with lightweight fusible interfacing (to stop the fabric fraying) and hand-sew them to the cloud, using blanket stitch (see page 133) for a neat finish.

APPLIQUÉ ADVICE
The absolute first rule is to test the stitch and practice on scrap project fabrics before starting sewing the real thing. Cut a shape with a wavy edge from cotton fabric and baste it to a piece of fur. Set the sewing machine to a zigzag stitch width of 3 and a stitch length of 0.5: these are the settings I used on my machine, but you can tweak them if your stitching doesn't look right. Put the fabric under the presser foot with the cotton wavy edge running under the middle of the foot. Turn the hand wheel to lower the needle and make one stitch to see where the needle is going in to the fabrics. If necessary, move the fabric under the foot so that when the needle comes down to the right it just misses the edge of the cotton and goes into the fur. Practice stitching slowly and carefully along the wavy edge. If you need to stop, always do so with the needle down in the fur; this will keep the stitched outline smooth.

5 | Follow Steps 2–4 to pin, baste, and stitch the sunray shapes on the other cloud piece.

6 | Pin the two cloud shapes right sides together. Taking a ⅝-in (1.5-cm) seam allowance, sew around the edges, leaving a gap of about 6in (15cm) in the bottom edge. Set the sewing machine to a wide zigzag and zigzag the seam allowances together all around (apart from across the open gap) for extra strength.

7 | Turn the cloud right side out through the gap, stuff it, then ladder stitch (see page 134) the gap closed.

Cat in a sweater,
NOT IN A HAT

A good companion for the snoozy dog (see page 26), this breed of cat might not be fat, but they are heavy and so perfectly adapted to their task of holding your door open. Made from recycled clothes and scraps of fabric, they are both thrifty and fabulous, and though their eyes might look glitteringly complicated, actually almost all of it is just stuff sewn on; there's minimal embroidery to do. And you can make your cat with different colored eyes using buttons for the centers and adding beads instead of sequins, if you prefer.

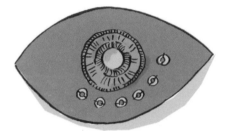

1 Enlarge the template by 200 per cent and cut out an eye. Use this eye template to cut two eyes from felt. I made slightly different designs on my cat's eyes, so he's sort of winking, but you can make your eyes identical, if you prefer. Start by sewing the mirror into the center of each eye using the gold thread. Then sew on sequins and/or embroider in chain stitch (see page 134) around the mirrors. I sewed on each sequin using two tiny straight stitches.

YOU'RE GOING TO NEED...
- Cat head template on page 142
- Paper for template
- Paper and fabric scissors
- Two pieces of fabric, each measuring 9in (23cm) square: I used corduroy from an old shirt
- Two pieces of felt, each measuring 3½ x 2in (9 x 5cm)
- Two gold shisha mirrors
- Tiny gold sequins
- Gold embroidery thread
- Embroidery needle
- Tiny button
- Old woolen sweater, felted (see Felting A Sweater, right)
- Pins
- Sewing threads to match fabrics
- Sewing machine
- Iron and ironing board
- Hand-sewing needle

- Basting thread: I always use ordinary sewing thread in a contrast color
- Piece of cotton fabric measuring 8 x 4in (20 x 10cm)
- Dried lentils
- Toy stuffing

FELTING A SWEATER
If you have a beautiful sweater—or cardigan, or tank—that you have inadvertently ruined by hot-washing it, then this is the perfect way to give it a new lease of life. If you're more careful with your laundry than that (I am, nowadays...), then you'll need to hunt for a sweater to ruin. The sweater needs to be 100 percent wool that hasn't been treated to make it machine washable: check the label and if it says "wash by hand," or "cool temperature wash," then you're good to go. And it's even better if it has a deep, ribbed welt.

You can felt in the washing machine, but I prefer to do it by hand as I get more control over the result: an overly-felted sweater can be too thick and stiff to make a nice cat from. You're

going to need a sink, hot water, cold water, rubber gloves, laundry detergent, and about 45 minutes. Firstly, fill the sink with the hottest running water available. Put on the gloves (to avoid scalding your hands), and mix into the hot water as much detergent as you'd use for a washer-load of laundry. Plunge the sweater into the water and start rubbing it between your hands. Rub one section, then move on to the next to felt it as evenly as possible all over. After about 30 minutes it should have thickened and the stitches blurred as the wool has felted. Drain the sink and fill it with cold water, then rinse the sweater thoroughly. If it isn't felted to your liking, then repeat the process.

If all that sounds like too much hard work (though it's very good for toning the upper arms), put the sweater in an old pillowcase (to avoid fibers clogging your washing machine), throw it in a hot wash, and cross your fingers.

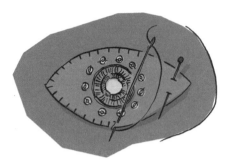

2 Using the head template, cut two heads from fabric. Position the eyes on one head on the right side of the fabric and pin them in place. Blanket stitch (see page 133) right around each eye using gold thread.

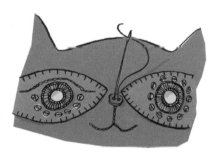

3 Following the template and using the photograph as a guide, embroider the mouth in gold chain stitch, then sew on the tiny button for the nose.

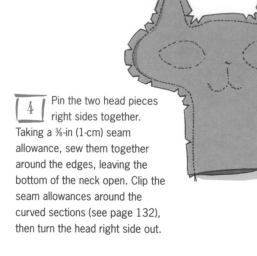

4 | Pin the two head pieces right sides together. Taking a ⅜-in (1-cm) seam allowance, sew them together around the edges, leaving the bottom of the neck open. Clip the seam allowances around the curved sections (see page 132), then turn the head right side out.

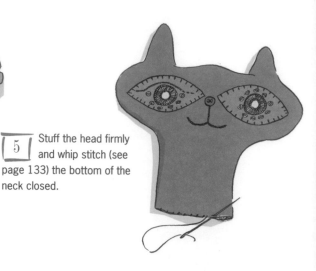

5 | Stuff the head firmly and whip stitch (see page 133) the bottom of the neck closed.

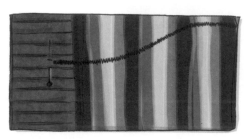

6 | Cut a piece of sweater, including a section of ribbed welt, measuring about 12¾ x 12in (32 x 30cm). Fold it in half right sides together and pin, placing a pin halfway down the welt and 4in (10cm) from the fold. Set the sewing machine to a tight zigzag stitch and sew a gently curving line from the outside edge of the bottom up to the pin, as shown.

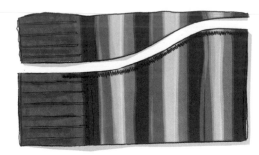

7 | Cut off the excess fabric, cutting straight up from the top of the line of stitching to the top of the welt.

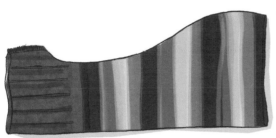

8 Turn the sweater right side out, then sew up the open part of the welt using a tight zigzag stitch as before. Test that the cat sweater welt fits snugly around the cat's neck, and take it in a bit more if need be.

9 Cut a circle of felted sweater measuring 4in (10cm) in diameter. Turn the tube of cat sweater wrong side out again, and pin the circle into the base. Ease the two pieces to fit; you may find it easiest to quickly baste the circle in place, rather than trying to sew with all the sticking-out pins. Using the tight zigzag stitch as before, sew the base in place. Turn the cat sweater right side out.

10 Fold the piece of cotton fabric in half and machine-sew the sides to make a small bag, leaving part of one side open. Fill the bag with dried lentils, packing in as many as you can, then hand-sew the gap closed.

11 Push the bag of lentils into the bottom of the cat sweater and pack in stuffing around it so that it's held firmly in place. Try to keep the base of the cat sweater as flat as possible. Stuff the sweater firmly up to the welt. Fold the welt over in half, then fold the top layer back up on itself. Push the cat's neck into the sweater and pin it in place through the single underlayer of the welt into the neck. If need be, add more stuffing to keep the cat's head from drooping.

12 Thread a needle with sewing thread, double it, and knot the ends. Sewing about halfway up the underlayer of the welt, backstitch (see page 133) the welt to the neck all around. Make the stitches go deeply into the neck so that the head is very firmly attached to the sweater (these cats tend to get picked up by their pointy ears, and you don't want the head coming off in your hand...). Fold the top layer of the welt down to cover the stitching.

Groovalicious
PATCHWORK

I've always liked the principle and potential of log cabin quilt blocks, but been put off by the formality and neatness. But wandering through Pinterest one day, I saw a fabulous version of a log cabin and so, rather late in the day, I came to know the ladies of Gees Bend. Do you know them? If not, look them up: they may be grandmas, but this ain't your grandma's quilting. The complexity of some of these deceptively simple-looking quilts is awesome. This wonky, single block log cabin is my simplified homage to the ladies.

YOU'RE GOING TO NEED...

- Fabrics; see How Much Fabric?, below
- Rotary cutter, ruler, and cutting mat
- Iron and ironing board
- Pins
- Sewing threads to match fabrics
- Sewing machine
- Quilter's rule, pattern square, or large set square
- Hand-sewing needle
- Sew-on patch/es (optional)
- Batting measuring 60½ x 69in (153 x 175cm): I used 100 percent cotton batting
- Quilter's safety pins (optional)

HOW MUCH FABRIC?

This is an extremely flexible quilt design, utterly perfect for using up bits from your fabric stash. Although you do need some quite long strips for the outer logs, they can be pieced: you can piece different patterns into a single strip, but I chose not to as I wanted to keep the log cabin shape clear. If you are buying fabrics, go for skinny quarters (a quarter yard/meter cut across the full width of the roll) rather than fat quarters (a measured yard/meter cut vertically then horizontally to make four pieces), so you'll have less piecing to do.

The finished size of this quilt is 56½ x 65in (143 x 165cm), but you can easily make a larger or smaller version by changing the size of the central rectangle and adding more or fewer logs around it. The size of the central rectangle here is 12 x 16in (30 x 40cm) and there are six logs above it, six to the right, five below it, and five to the left (this is because I made five and a half tiers of logs to get to the quilt size I wanted, rather than completing the last tier: so scold me!). My logs vary from 1¼in (3cm) to 9in (23cm) wide. And I sewed this quilt with ⅜-in (1-cm) seam allowances, rather than the traditional ¼in (6mm), because the design is simple and spacious and so the seams wouldn't be creating too much bulk.

For the quilt backing: a piece of fabric measuring 60½ x 69in (153 x 175cm), or several pieces joined to make a backing this size

For the binding: a strip measuring 7¾yd (7.1m) long by 3¾in (9.5cm) wide: this is 23½in (60cm) of 55-in (140-cm) wide fabric, or 28in (70cm) of 44-in (112-cm) wide fabric, including extra for joining strips (see Step 11).

1 Cut a central rectangle of fabric that is more or less in scale to the size you want the finished quilt to be: this piece was 12 x 16in (30 x 40cm). Using a ruler and rotary cutter and cutting mat, cut an angled sliver off one short end. Don't make it too angled or you'll set up problems for the next stage: this sliver is about ⅛in (3mm) at the thin end and ⅝in (1.5cm) at the wide end. Pin a safety pin through the fabric close to the top edge so that you'll always know where the top of the block is.

2 Start the first tier of logs at the top of the block. Cut a strip the desired width and a bit longer than the width of the central rectangle. Right sides together, pin it to the top of the rectangle, letting it overlap a bit at each end.

3 Taking a ⅜-in (1-cm) seam allowance, sew the pieces together. Open them out and press the seam allowances toward the central rectangle.

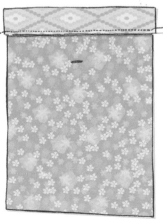

4 Using a ruler and rotary cutter, trim off the ends of the strip to align with the edges of the central rectangle.

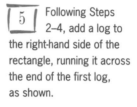 

5 Following Steps 2–4, add a log to the right-hand side of the rectangle, running it across the end of the first log, as shown.

6 Continue in this way until you've added a whole tier of logs. At this stage, just ignore the fact that one edge of the rectangle isn't square.

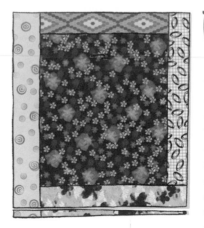

7 Now, before adding the next tier of logs, you need to square this tier up. I cut the angled strip off the bottom of the rectangle in Step 1, so that's the edge that needs squaring. Use a quilter's rule, a pattern square (my choice), or if all else fails a large set square, to square off that edge in relation to the rest of the block and cut off the excess.

8 | Having made the block square, you need to make it wonky again, but on a different edge. Slice off an angle as in Step 1. This is a steeper angle than before, but the logs must always be a minimum of ¾in (2cm) wide to allow for seaming. You need to always square up and re-wonk the block after each tier of logs, or the wonkiness will quickly grow out of easy control.

9 | Starting at the top of the block again, follow Steps 2–8 to add more tiers of logs until the quilt is the size you want.

10 | I stitched on a sugar skull embroidered patch: you can add any such embellishments you want, if you want.

11 | Then follow Steps 8–9 of Geektastic Quilt (see pages 20–21) to make the sandwich, and Step 10 to quilt the tiers of logs in the ditch. Follow Steps 11–19 on pages 21–22 to finish and bind the quilt.

$\mathcal{H}exie$
CUSHION

I've always loved the principles of hexie patchwork; the re-use of scraps of delicious fabrics, the methodical construction, the neat hand-stitching, the portability of the blocks—just the perfect craft for trains, planes, and automobiles. For this cushion I've gone for a classy two-color palette to balance out the eccentric fringing, but dial up the craziness and use a jumble of colors if that works for you. And it's quite small—13½in (34cm) in diameter—to keep it doable in the foreseeable future (hexie patchwork is a little slow, though for me that's one of its pleasures), but you could make a larger cushion simply by making larger hexies.

YOU'RE GOING TO NEED...
- Hexie templates (see page 143)
- Paper
- Fabric and paper scissors
- Pins
- 19 scraps of fabric measuring at least 3⅓in (8.5cm) square
- Basting thread: I always use ordinary sewing thread in a contrast color
- Hand-sewing needle
- Sewing threads to match fabrics
- Two pieces of medium-weight fabric at least 14in (36cm) square: I used calico
- Compasses, or a 13½-in (34-cm) diameter dinner plate to use as a template
- Sewing machine
- Iron and ironing board
- Scraps of ribbons and yarns: I used four different ribbons and three knitting yarns
- Stuffing: see Step 15

MAKING THE HEXIE BLOCK

1 Carefully draw around the smaller (inner) template 19 times onto paper. Cut out these hexagons VERY ACCURATELY. The success of your patchwork depends a lot on these shapes being precise. Then draw around the larger (outer) template onto the wrong side of the pieces of fabric. Cut out these fabric hexies, though you don't have to be as accurate as you were for the papers.

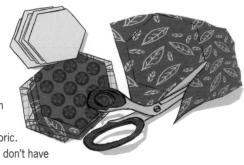

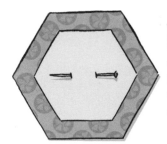

2 Thread a sewing needle—the finest you are comfortable with—and knot one end of the thread. Do this now so it's to hand when you need it. Pin a paper to the wrong side of one of the fabric pieces, centering it as accurately as you can.

TO KNOT OR NOT TO KNOT
In a perfect world there are no knots in patchwork (apart from the basting knots). Start a seam a short way in from the corner, sew along to the corner, then sew back over these stitches and along the seam. Secure the thread by stitching back along the seam a short way. If that sounds a bit much, just start with a knot: the world isn't perfect.

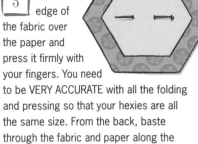

3 Fold one edge of the fabric over the paper and press it firmly with your fingers. You need to be VERY ACCURATE with all the folding and pressing so that your hexies are all the same size. From the back, baste through the fabric and paper along the folded edge, bringing the needle though to the back again a short distance before the corner.

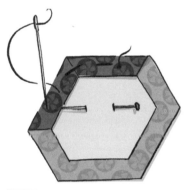

4 Fold over the adjacent edge of the fabric and finger-press it firmly, making sure that the corner is neat and sharp. Do not pull the fabric too tight or you will distort the shape of the patch. Baste along that folded edge.

5 Continue in this way right around the hexagon, folding over, pressing, and basting each edge in turn. Secure the end of the thread with a couple of backstitches through the first folded edge, stitching through the fabric only. Remove the pin. Make 18 more hexies...

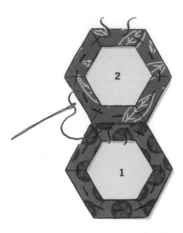

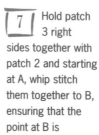

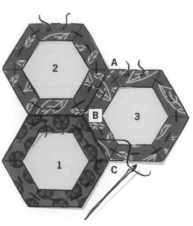

6 | Choose a hexie for the center and hold it right sides together with another patch, matching the edges. Using tiny whip stitches (see page 133), sew the patches together along one edge. (This illustration shows the patches flat so you can see the seam, and the patch labeled "1" is the center patch.) The stitches should go through just the very edge of the fabric, not through the paper.

7 | Hold patch 3 right sides together with patch 2 and starting at A, whip stitch them together to B, ensuring that the point at B is stitched precisely to the corner between 1 and 2. Then fold 3 so that it is right sides together with 1 (sounds tricky but it isn't, just try to crease the fabric as little as possible), and whip stitch from B to C.

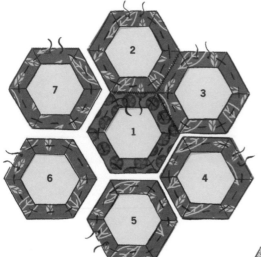

8 | Sew four more patches around the central patch in the same way as in Step 7, sewing each one to an edge of the previous patch and then to an edge of the central patch, and fitting them in as shown.

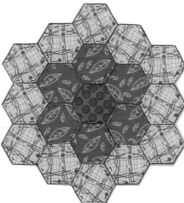

9 | Then add another ring of 12 patches in the same way to complete the block.

10 | Press the block, then take out the basting stitches and all the papers. Do the edge patches last and do them carefully to avoid pulling on the fabric and distorting the shape, which is quite easily done (listen to the voice of bitter experience here). Baste the folded outer edges in place all round the completed patchwork.

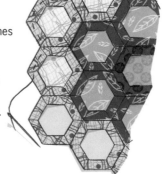

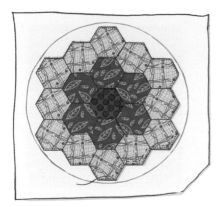

MAKING THE CUSHION

11 Draw a 13½-in (34-cm) circle on one piece of calico, but don't cut it out. Pin and then baste the hexie block centrally onto the circle, making sure it is flat and smooth. You can either hand- or machine-sew the block in place. I machine-sewed, topstitching ⅛in (3mm) in from the edge of the block and pivoting at all the corners. If you hand-sew, you can either whip stitch or blanket stitch (see page 133) around the edges. Remove the basting stitches from the outer edge of the patchwork.

12 The fringe was inspired by the idea of patchwork and is pretty much a make-it-up-as-you-go-along item. Cut lengths of ribbon about 3in (8cm) long and fold lengths of yarn into similar-sized loops. Using a straight stitch, machine-sew very slowly along the drawn line on the cushion front, feeding the loops of ribbon and yarn under the needle as you go. The loops must face inward, toward the center of the cushion, with the cut ends just protruding beyond the line. Make a few stitches to hold a loop in place, then stop with the needle down and arrange the next loop/s butted up to the previous one, and sew over those. Continue right around the cushion. If you feel the fringe is not thick enough, you can make a second row of stitching over the first one and add more loops in thin patches.

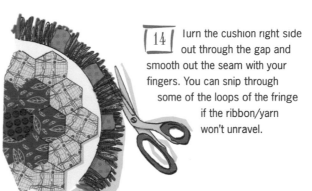

13 On the wrong side of the second piece of fabric, draw a 13½in (34cm) circle and a concentric circle ⅜in (1cm) larger. Cut out around the larger circle. Lay this right side down on top of the fringed front and pin it in place, carefully matching the drawn inner line with the line of stitching holding the fringe. Stitching just a tiny amount inside the drawn line, sew the front and back together, leaving a small gap.

14 Turn the cushion right side out through the gap and smooth out the seam with your fingers. You can snip through some of the loops of the fringe if the ribbon/yarn won't unravel.

15 Fill the cushion and ladder stitch (see page 134) the gap closed. I like feather cushions, so I raided an old square cushion for feathers to fill this one: what a nightmare! There were feathers everywhere and the only happy creatures were the cats. But once I had vacuumed me, the room, and the cushion, I liked the result, so maybe it was worth it.

Under
CANVAS...

Yo-yo-a-go-go

YOU'RE GOING TO NEED...

- Template on page 138
- Paper for templates
- Paper scissors and fabric scissors
- Two pieces of main fabric and two pieces of lining fabric, each measuring 20 x 14in (50 x 35cm): I used medium-weight cotton, but you can use anything reasonably sturdy
- Fabrics for yo-yos: I used 6in (15cm), 8in (20cm), and 9½in (24cm) circles for the gathered parts and 3¾in (9cm), 5in (13cm), and 6in (15cm) circles for the contrast inners: I used lightweight cotton, you don't want anything thick or the yo-yos won't gather nicely
- Fusible webbing the size of the contrast inner circles
- Iron and ironing board
- Sewing threads to match fabrics
- Hand-sewing needle
- Sewing machine with free-motion embroidery function (if you want to do the embroidery...)
- Variegated machine embroidery thread (see above...)
- Pins
- Decorative buttons (if you want them...)
- 8in (20cm) zipper: I used a chunky vintage one with a big metal ring that I can hang up my bag from

Both a stash buster and a stash holder: how good can a simple bag get? One thing that all campers need is storage to stash their stuff in and keep a tiny tent tidy, so make as many bags as you need to organize your unmentionables, wash kit, pjs, wooly hat and scarf (just in case)... This is a big bag, but you can make yours any size you like. The yo-yos are optional—without them you can whiz up a bag in under half-an-hour—but they are rather lovely, and really much easier to make than they might look (check out the **EXCELLENT NEWS** bits in the steps).

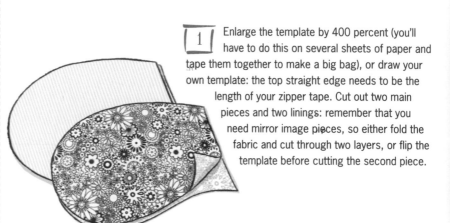

1 Enlarge the template by 400 percent (you'll have to do this on several sheets of paper and tape them together to make a big bag), or draw your own template: the top straight edge needs to be the length of your zipper tape. Cut out two main pieces and two linings: remember that you need mirror image pieces, so either fold the fabric and cut through two layers, or flip the template before cutting the second piece.

TO MAKE THE YO-YOS

2 Cut circles of fusible webbing the size you want the finished yo-yos to be and iron them on to the back of the pieces of contrast inner fabric. Cut out all the circles you'll need.

YO-YO SIZES
Remember that a yo-yo will be the size of the smaller, inner circle; it's easiest to work out the sizes and positions you want for the yo-yos by placing just the smaller circles on the bag piece and taking a photo, before ironing the circles onto the larger ones.

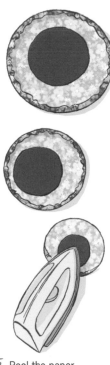

3 Peel the paper backing off the webbing and iron a small circle onto the wrong side of each larger circle. You can position the small circles off-center, as here, but make sure that they are at least 1in (2.5cm) from the edge of their big circle. Press under a very narrow hem all around the edge of each large circle. **EXCELLENT NEWS**: these hems don't have to be even as it doesn't matter if your circle is less than perfectly circular.

4 I embellished the middle of my yo-yos by scribbling on them with free-motion embroidery and variegated thread. You could leave yours plain, use a print fabric, use hand-embroidery stitches (see pages 133–136), sew on buttons or patches; whatever you want really.

5 Using a long length of doubled sewing thread, work a row of running stitches around the hem of each circle, starting and ending on the right side. **MORE EXCELLENT NEWS**: the stitches don't need to be even or neat, though they shouldn't be too long—about ¼in (6mm) is good. Leave a long tail of thread hanging free at the end of the stitches.

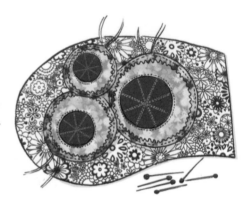

6 Pin the yo-yos onto the bag front piece: it doesn't matter if the larger circles overlap. Set the sewing machine to a small straight stitch (if you did machine embroidery in Step 4, remember to raise the feed dogs), and sew around the edge of each smaller circle. **YET MORE EXCELLENT NEWS**: the stitched circles don't have to sit smoothly against the fabric circles, or be perfectly round.

7 One yo-yo at a time, pull on the tail of the gathering thread (the one you left hanging free in Step 5) and the starting knot end to gather up the edge of the yo-yo. Even out the gathers a bit (**ANOTHER PIECE OF EXCELLENT NEWS**: it doesn't matter if the gathers aren't THAT even), and make sure that the inner circle is lying flat. (If you pull up the gathers too tight, the inner circle will bunch up and the bag piece won't lie flat.) Tie the tail and knot end together in a firm double knot.

8 Thread the ends of the gathering threads into a needle and take them down through a trough in the gathers to the back and secure them there with a few backstitches. But don't cut the threads just yet: stab stitch (see page 136) around the edge of the gathered circle, taking the needle up and down in a gather trough every ¾in (2cm) or so, to hold the gathered edge flat against the bag. This isn't vital, especially on small yo-yos, but it does help larger ones to sit neatly.

9 I sewed buttons into the center of my yo-yos using fly stitch: bring the needle up through one buttonhole and down through another, but don't pull the thread tight. Bring the needle up beyond the edge of the button, between the positions of the two holes, and take it through the loop of thread. Pull the thread taut, then make a short straight stitch to finish the fly stitch (see also page 134). I used four-hole buttons and made four fly stitches, so that each button is held down by a stitched star. I also sewed some orange buttons to the centers of some of the printed flowers on the bag fabric.

TO MAKE UP THE BAG

10 Bits of the next few steps might seem complicated, but take it slowly and all will be well. Lay the decorated bag front piece face up, and lay the zipper face down on top of it, so that all of the zipper is lying on the fabric with the edge of one tape against the top edge of the fabric. Lay a lining piece face down on top, matching the edges to the front bag piece. Pin and then baste the pieces together along the upper zipper tape.

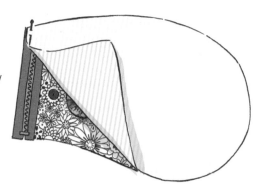

11 Fit a zipper foot to the sewing machine and sew along the basted tape. You can sew as near to the teeth as you want: I like the exposed zipper look, so I sewed quite close to the outer edge of the tape.

12 Fold the lining and main fabric wrong sides together, so that the zipper sticks out, as shown. Press the seam flat.

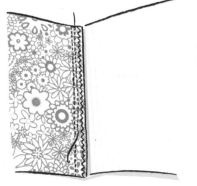

13 Open the lining and main fabric out again and zigzag along the seam allowance (for extra strength). Then fold the seam allowance flat against the lining, and sew a line of straight stitch about ⅛in (3mm) below the seam line, understitching the lining to the seam allowance. This will help stop the lining getting caught in the zipper when you open the bag. Fold the lining and main fabric right sides together again, and give the seam another quick press.

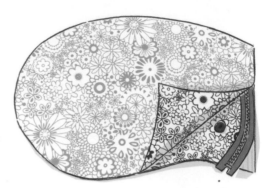

14 To sew the bag back and lining to the other zipper tape, first lay the back lining flat and face up. Lay the front bag and lining (treat them as one piece), face up on top, positioning the free edge of the zipper tape against the top edge of the back lining. Then lay the bag back on top, matching the edges to the back lining. Pin and then baste the pieces together along the free zipper tape. Follow Steps 11–13 to sew the fabric pieces to the zipper.

15 When you open the bag pieces out, it should look like a (rather peculiar) butterfly, with the zipper as its body. Undo the zipper halfway; this is vital.

16 Fold the bag pieces together, linings facing out. Using sewing thread, whip stitch (see page 133) the ends of the tapes together, at each end of the zipper.

17 Open the bag out so that the linings are right sides together, as are the main pieces: the zipper will be invisible. Pin the layers together right around the edges. Take time to make sure the zipper tapes are neatly folded down toward the lining; if they are a bit unruly it's worth basting them. Starting near the bottom of the lining, sew right around the edge of the whole shape, leaving a 4in (10cm) gap in the lining.

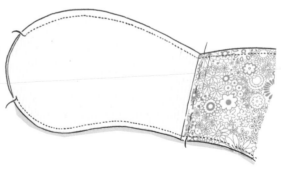

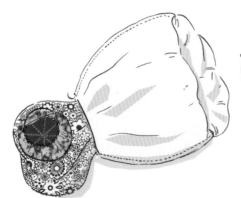

18 Reach in through the gap in the lining and carefully pull the main bag through the half-opened zipper (now you see why it was vital!), and carry on pulling it right through the gap in the lining. Continue pulling until the lining is right side out, too. Press the seams flat, pressing under the seam allowances across the gap in the lining, then ladder stitch (see page 134) the gap closed. Tuck the lining inside the bag and you're done.

Keep
STUFF SAFE #1

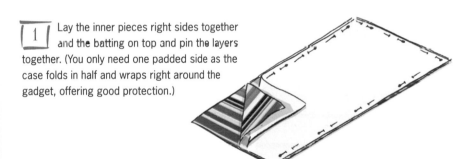

YOU'RE GOING TO NEED...

- Two pieces of waterproof outer fabric and two pieces of soft inner fabric, one piece of batting, two pieces of twill tape: see Size Matters, below (and don't freak out at all the numbers, it's quite simple math, really)
- Fabric scissors
- Iron and ironing board
- Pins
- Sewing threads to match fabrics
- Sewing machine
- Hand-sewing needle

SIZE MATTERS

Measure the length, width, and depth of the gadget. Cut two pieces of inner fabric and one piece of batting each measuring the length plus the depth plus 1¼in (3cm), by the width multiplied by two plus the depth plus 1½in (4cm). Cut two pieces of outer fabric ¼in (5mm) larger than the inner pieces. Cut two pieces of tape the length of the outers.

For example, my tablet is 9¾in (24.5cm) long, 7¼in (18.5cm) wide, and ⅜in (1cm) deep.

So my pieces of inner fabric and batting are: 11⅜in (28.5cm) x 16⅝in (42cm)

Length: 9¾in (24.5cm) + ⅜in (1cm) + 1¼in (3cm) = 11⅜in (28.5cm)

Width: 7¼in (18.5cm) x 2 + ⅜in (1cm) + 1½in (4cm) = 16⅝in (42cm)

And my outer pieces are 11½in (29cm) by 16⅝in (42.5cm)

And my pieces of tape are 16⅞in (42.5cm) long

When we weren't looking, technology crept out of the office and leapt right into our everyday lives: e-reader, tablet, MP3 player, laptop, cell phone—most of us have one or more about our person at all times, and it's wise to give them a bit of extra protection if they are coming camping with you. This easy-to-make case is padded and water-resistant (note "resistant," not "proof;" don't take it to a mud bath and expect it to work wonders), and can be scaled to suit whatever box of tricks you want to keep safe.

1. Lay the inner pieces right sides together and the batting on top and pin the layers together. (You only need one padded side as the case folds in half and wraps right around the gadget, offering good protection.)

2. Taking a ⅜-in (1-cm) seam allowance, sew down one long edge, pivot at the corner and sew a third of the way along the bottom short edge. Repeat on the opposite edge, so that the top short edge is open and the bottom has a gap in the middle. Leave this piece wrong side out. Trim the bottom corners.

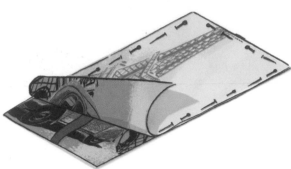

3 | Sew one end of each piece of tape to the opposite edges of the outer front, on the right side and centering them on the short edges. Lay the outer back right side down on top of the front, matching the raw edges. Pin the pieces together, making sure the free ends of tape are tucked away from the edges.

4 | Taking a ⅜-in (1-cm) seam allowance, sew right around the two long edges and the bottom short edge. Turn the outer right side out, pulling the tapes free. Fold over and hem the ends of the tapes if they have a tendency to unravel.

5 | With the padded side of the inner uppermost and the outer right side up, slide the outer into the inner, so that the two pieces are right sides together. Match the raw top edges and make sure that the free ends of tape are tucked down inside.

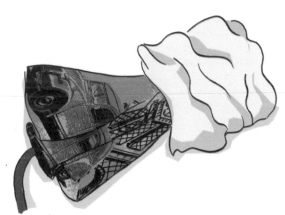

6 | Taking a ⅜-in (1-cm) seam allowance, sew right around the top edge, easing the inner a bit to fit the outer as you sew.

7 | Turn the whole thing right side out by pulling it through the gap in the bottom of the inner. Pull the outer through, then keep pulling until the inner is right side out as well.

Oversew the gap in the inner closed, then tuck it inside the outer, pushing out the corners neatly. Slip the gadget inside and fold the case in half, padded side out, and wrap the tapes around and tie them.

Do away
WITH DAMP

There are only three not-lovely things about camping, and a damp derrière is one of them. (Since you ask, small flying things that bite and erratic facilities are the others.) Thankfully, damp unmentionables are easily averted with a practical but also deeply gorgeous mat. The waterproof backing is topped with patchwork: I've included some crochet granny squares in my version, but yours can be just as perfect made entirely from fabric.

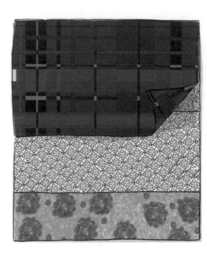

1 The way to make up the patchwork top is to sew together pieces into strips and then join these in rows. So, the patches in each strip need to be the same width, but can be different lengths. Stagger the horizontal seams in adjacent strips to reduce bulk. Cut two patches to the same width and pin them right sides together. Sew the seam taking a ⅜-in (1-cm) seam allowance, and press the seam open. Repeat to make a strip of patches.

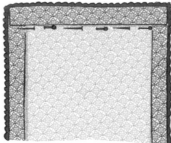

2 If you are incorporating granny squares into your mat, then they will determine the width of the strips they are in. The pattern (see page 137) has an extra round of single (double) crochet around the edge, and this acts as a seam allowance. I found it easiest to press under the seam allowances of fabric patches to be joined to crochet squares, then I could see to position the edge of the fabric in the right place on the crochet and pin the pieces together. Open the seam allowances out and sew the seam along the pressed line.

3 | If you pin and sew carefully, the seam will be very neat on the crochet squares as well as the fabric. Avoid having a crochet square on any edges of the mat, as the binding (see Step 6) will intrude into the pattern.

4 | Sew the strips together to make the patchwork mat top. When you are sewing, you might find it easiest to have strips with crochet squares uppermost, then you can see to sew across them in the right place.

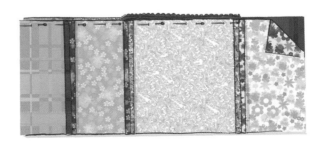

5 Lay the patchwork mat top on the waterproof backing, wrong sides together. Smooth the top flat and pin the layers together close to the edge: don't put pins elsewhere in the mat or its waterproofness will be compromised and a damp derrière will creep in. Trim any excess fabric from the patchwork to fit the backing, then sew right around the edge, ¼in (6mm) in, to hold the layers together.

6 Press the cotton tape in half lengthwise. Starting a short distance before one corner, fold the tape over the edge of the mat and pin in place to the corner.

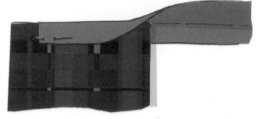

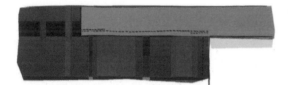

7 Stitching about ¼in (6mm) from the edge, sew up to the corner, reversing at the start and end of the stitching to secure it.

8 Fold the tape around the corner to make a neat miter. Pin and then sew the tape in place right along to the next corner. Repeat at every corner to bind the edges of the whole mat.

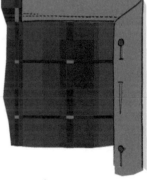

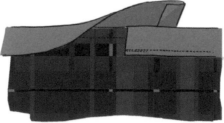

9 Before sewing the last edge, fold ⅜in (1cm) of the end of the tape under, trimming off any excess as needed, and lap it over the starting point. Pin in place, then sew the tape, sewing right over the folded end.

UNDER CANVAS...

Star

STRUCK

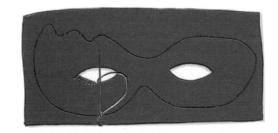

YOU'RE GOING TO NEED...

- Mask template on page 142
- Paper for template
- Paper, fabric, and small sharp embroidery scissors
- Piece of felt, piece of cotton fabric, and piece of fusible webbing each measuring at least 8¾ x 4¾in (22 x 12cm)
- Water-soluble fabric marker
- Embroidery flosses: I used perlé cottons
- Embroidery and beading needles
- Beading thread
- Small beads and sequins: I used metallic delica beads and tiny star sequins
- Scraps of fabric and fusible webbing
- Iron and ironing board
- Baking parchment or greaseproof paper
- Two pieces of 1-in (2.5-cm) wide organza ribbon, each about 20in (50cm) long

Add glamour to your festival look, while avoiding the faff of eye make-up, by wearing big sunglasses during the day and a carnival mask at night. Instant color and sparkle for the evening (and a useful cover-up for eye bags after a day or so of late partying and poor sleep). A mask is easy to make to match

any outfit, and as this version is lined with cotton, it's smooth against your skin so you can wear it all night, if need be... I've stitched stars on to my mask, but you can add whatever embellishments you like.

1 Enlarge the mask template by 200 percent and cut out the outline and eyeholes. Draw around the template onto the right side of the felt, then, using the small sharp scissors, cut out just the eyeholes (it's easier to decorate the mask before cutting it out, and there's less risk of stretching the felt).

2 Using embroidery floss, work blanket stitch (see page 133) around the edge of each eyehole. Dodge the need to do this neatly and evenly by making the legs of the stitches deliberately different lengths.

3 Use the fabric marker to draw decorative shapes onto your mask: I've gone for stars, but anything that fits the space and that you can embroider is good. Embroider the motifs you've drawn. I've used simple running stitch (see page 135) to work my stars.

4 Add beads and sequins to the embroidery. I've sewn on beads between several of the running stitches, and a sequin topped by a bead at the center of each star.

5 Cut out the mask outline and remove any remaining fabric marker marks with a damp cloth.

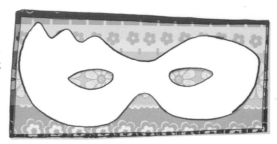

6 Iron the fusible webbing onto the back of the piece of cotton fabric. Lay the template right side up on the back of the fabric and cut the fabric very roughly to shape.

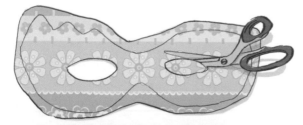

7 Using the small sharp scissors, cut out the eyeholes from the cotton fabric, cutting just outside the drawn line so that they will be a little larger than the eyeholes in the felt.

8 Lay the embroidered felt right side down on the baking parchment. Peel the paper backing off the fusible webbing and place the cotton fabric right side up on top of the felt, carefully aligning the eyeholes in both pieces. Iron the cotton with a hot iron to bond it to the back of the felt. Carefully peel the whole mask off the baking parchment; the fusible webbing from the excess cotton fabric may come off a bit onto the parchment, so be sure not to get any of it on the decorated felt.

| 9 | Carefully cut out the cotton around the edge of the felt mask.

| 10 | At either end of the mask, on the cotton, iron on a piece of fusible webbing measuring about ¾ x ⅜in (2 x 1cm). Iron small pieces of webbing onto the back of scraps of fabric, then cut out two circles, each measuring about 1in (2.5cm) in diameter. Peel the paper backing off all the webbing.

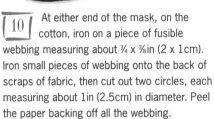

| 11 | Lay one end of a piece of ribbon on a piece of the webbing on the mask, then lay a fabric circle right side up over the end of the ribbon. Protecting the ribbon itself with a cloth, iron the circles to bond the ribbon firmly to the mask. Repeat on the other side of the mask.

Home

IS OVER THERE

YOU'RE GOING TO NEED...

- One piece of fabric measuring 12 x 14¼in (30 x 36cm), one piece measuring 12 x 10½in (30 x 27cm), and one piece measuring 12 x 6¾in (30 x 17cm): see What Fabrics?, below
- Pins
- Sewing threads to match fabrics
- Sewing machine
- Iron and ironing board
- Ruler
- Fading fabric marker
- Rotary cutter and cutting mat, or fabric scissors
- 69in (175cm) of ¾-in (2-cm) wide bias binding
- Flagpole: I have an extendable one that I strongly suspect was originally made to be a fishing pole

WHAT FABRICS?

You want your flag to be lightweight and reversible, so a fabric that's got visible pattern on both sides is best. And your flag will get wet at some point, so make it from something that won't shrink or mark, and will dry quickly: I've used cotton gingham in three different check sizes. The sizes of my pieces were determined in part by the gingham pattern, but you can use the same principles to make a larger or smaller flag (not too small or you'll never see it).

I didn't take a distinctive flag—or any flag for that matter—to my first ever festival, and as a result spent a considerable amount of time looking for my tent after watching a band (Tibetan Ukranian Mountain Troupe, in case you were wondering; which does rather date the event…). Fortunately, I had a more experienced neighbor and subsequently navigated by their flag, but I made my own before the next festival. Here is a sturdy and easy-to-make pennant that you can hoist high and home in on.

1 Pin the largest and middle size pieces of fabric together, wrong sides facing, centering the 10½in (27cm) edge of the middle piece on the 14¼in (36cm) edge of the large piece. Taking a ⅝-in (1.5-cm) seam allowance, sew the two pieces together. To make flat fell seams (for a strong and neat finish), trim the seam allowance of the middle piece to half its original width.

 2 Fold the wider seam allowance over the narrower one, as shown, and press flat.

3 Open the joined pieces out flat and press the folded seam allowance toward the middle piece. Topstitch along the folded edge.

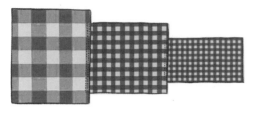

4 | Sew the smallest piece to the opposite edge of the middle piece in the same way, centering the small piece on the edge of the middle piece, as in Step 1.

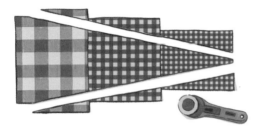

5 | Measure the diameter of the top of your flagpole and add ⅜in (1cm): this will make the channel that goes over the flagpole. Starting this distance in from the raw edge of the largest piece, and using a ruler and fabric marker, draw a pennant shape across the joined fabrics, as shown. Cut along the marked line. Don't cut to a sharp point; make it about ⅜in (1cm) square.

7 | Fold the binding neatly around the tip of the pennant, then sew it in place along the other slanting edge and finishing on the straight edge at the bottom of the channel.

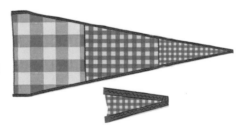

6 | Iron the bias binding in half lengthwise. Set the sewing machine to a narrow zigzag stitch. Starting at the straight edge at the top of the channel and working along one slanting edge, fold the binding over the edge of the fabric and zigzag stitch it in place. I sewed slowly and positioned the binding as I went, but you can pin it in place first if you find that easier.

8 | Turn under ⅜in (1cm) along the unbound straight edge, then fold the fabric over to form the channel. Using straight stitch, sew up the side and across the top of the channel. Slip the channel over the top of your flagpole. My pole has an eye at the tip and I made a few stitches through the flag and eye to keep them firmly together.

Looking groovy
WHATEVER THE WEATHER

(no relation to Lovely Clare, see page 72)

YOU'RE GOING TO NEED...
- Selection of lightweight cotton fabrics: see Shapes and Sizes, below
- Iron and ironing board
- Rotary cutter, ruler, and cutting mat, or fabric scissors
- Pins
- Sewing threads to match fabrics
- Sewing machine
- Point turner or chopstick
- ⅝-in (1.5-cm) wide bias binding the length you want the bunting to be, plus 8in (20cm): see Shapes and Sizes, below
- Pom-pom trim (optional)
- Scraps of ribbon (optional)

SHAPES AND SIZES
This is a great stash buster project; fabric pieces as small as 6in (15cm) square will make good pennants. And because the triangles are different sizes, you can use up oddly shaped leftovers from other projects. I used a single color palette, with checks, stripes, spots, and star patterns, but that's just my taste. My bunting is approximately 4yd (3.75m) long finished length, and has 12 pennants on it.

There's an art, a skill, a science… a something to camping in style. A guru of good-looking camping is Lovely Sarah (no relation to Lovely Clare, see page 72), who always, but always, has bunting up around her tent and gazebo. The bunting I've made here can be simplified if you're going away tomorrow—see **SUPER-SIMPLE BUNTING**—but the full version doesn't take long and will give you years of gleeful glamping.

1 Cut out half the number of pennants you want, the size and precise shape can be determined by the fabrics you have available. I cut 12 pennants: the smallest is 5¾in (14.5cm) wide and 7in (17.5cm) from top to tip, and the largest is 9½in (24cm) wide and 9in (23cm) from top to tip. I had gingham fabrics with three sizes of squares, so I cut all my first batch of pennants from these as that was the easiest way of making the patterns work neatly. For **SUPER-SIMPLE BUNTING**, cut out the pieces using pinking shears or a rotary cutter with a pinking blade.

2 Right sides together, pin the cut out pennants to other pieces of fabric. For **SUPER-SIMPLE BUNTING**, skip this step and the next three steps and go straight to Step 6.

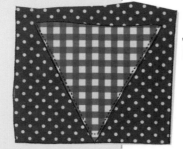

3 Taking ⅜-in (1-cm) seam allowances, machine sew the pennants to the fabric. Sew down one sloping side, lift the presser foot and pivot the fabric then make a couple of stitches straight across the pennant, then pivot the fabric again to sew up the other sloping side. This will help you make the neatest points. Leave the top straight edge unstitched.

4 Cut the pennants out, at the same time trimming the seam allowances to about ¼in (6mm) and cutting off the excess fabric at the point. A rotary cutter and ruler offer the quickest and easiest method of doing this.

5 Turn the pennants right side out, pushing out the point with a point turner or a knitting needle or chopstick. Press the pennants flat.

6 Iron the bias binding in half lengthwise. Lay it out flat (you'll probably need to do this on the floor) and space the pennants out along it. I spaced mine irregularly, making sure that adjacent pennants were different shapes, and that the different fabric patterns were evenly distributed. When you are happy with the arrangement, take a digital photo to refer back to. Stack the flags in a pile in the order in which you'll sew them to the binding (see Step 10).

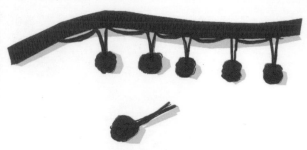

7   The pom-poms are very optional, but do add an extra jaunty note to the bunting. Cut individual pom-poms off a length of pom-pom trim, pulling out the linking cord as far as possible on each pom-pom before cutting it off: don't worry if the separate pom-poms end up with tails of different lengths, they can just hang at different heights. For **SUPER-SIMPLE BUNTING**, skip this bit.

8   Fold over 2in (5cm) at one end of the binding to make a loop (to hang the bunting by) and pin it in place.

9   Set the sewing machine to a medium zigzag stitch. Put the pinned end of the loop under the needle, making sure the open edge of the binding is facing to the left. Start zigzag stitching along the binding, sewing the loop in place, then reversing to secure the stitching and strengthen the loop. Zigzag along a short length then slip the tails of a pom-pom into the folded binding and zigzag over them. For **SUPER-SIMPLE BUNTING**, don't include the pom-poms.

10   Zigzag another short distance, then, referring back to your photo (or just winging it a bit, as I did), slip in the raw edges of the first pennant in your stack and zigzag over that. Continue in this way (I did alternate pom-poms and pennants) until you have about 6–8in (15–20cm) of binding left to sew. Fold over the last 2in (5cm) to make a loop and sew up to it, sewing down the end then reversing to secure the stitching and strengthen the loop.

11   For final (optional) perkiness, knot a scrap of ribbon around the binding between the tails of each pom-pom. For **SUPER-SIMPLE BUNTING**, skip this bit (obviously).

Keep stuff
SAFE #2

YOU'RE GOING TO NEED...

- Fabric and medium-weight fusible interfacing (see Customizing the Belt Design, below)
- Fabric scissors
- Iron and ironing board
- 6in (15cm) zipper
- Pins
- Hand-sewing needle
- Basting thread: I always use ordinary sewing thread in a contrast color
- Sewing threads to match fabrics
- Sewing machine
- Buckle or clasp (see Customizing The Belt Design, below)
- Masking tape
- Eyelets to fit buckle tongue (if you are using a buckle rather than a clasp)

CUSTOMIZING THE BELT DESIGN

The width of the belt is determined by the width of the part of the clasp or buckle that the fabric is attached to (see Step 7). So a narrow clasp will only give you a very skinny pocket. For a clasp, you need two strips of fabric and one of medium-weight fusible interfacing that measure the required width plus ¾in (2cm), by your waist measurement plus 4in (10cm).

I made my strips longer than this as my original purse belt had an adjustable slider and I wanted to use it on this belt, too.

If you're using a buckle, then the same width is needed, but you need extra length to thread through the buckle: experiment with your buckle and a strip of paper to see how much fabric you need.

My regulation school summer dresses were pink-and-white striped sacks with narrow collars, zipped-up fronts, and too-short sleeves: everyone, absolutely everyone, looked terrible in them. The amount of customizing that could be done was severely curtailed by strict uniform regulations, but one accessory that was permitted was a purse belt, though it did have to be maroon. At least it gave the sack a bit of shape. And you had somewhere to keep your candy money. And when I left school I kept the belt and wore it to festivals to keep cash safe. And when the belt fell apart, I kept the clasp, and that is the clasp on this belt. So it is worth hoarding the odd thing or two... See left for tips on altering this belt design to suit your own clasp or buckle.

1 Iron the interfacing onto the back of one of the fabric strips; this will be the outer side of the belt. Press under a ⅜-in (1-cm) hem along one long edge of each belt piece.

2 Position the zipper face down on the hem of the interfaced fabric, with the teeth of one tape aligned with the folded edge of the hem. If you are right-handed (as I am), then you want the zipper pull about 4in (10cm) from the right-hand end of the belt: the same distance from the left-hand end if you are left-handed. (I had to put the strip around my waist, right side out and folded hem uppermost, to work out where my zipper should go: I recommend the same procedure for safety.) Pin and then baste the tape in position.

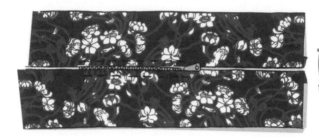

3 Making sure the ends of both strips are aligned, repeat the process to baste the folded edge of the other strip to the other zipper tape.

4 Fold the ends of the tapes away from the zipper teeth, as shown. Machine-sew close to the teeth on each side, sewing over the folded tapes, to sew the zipper in place.

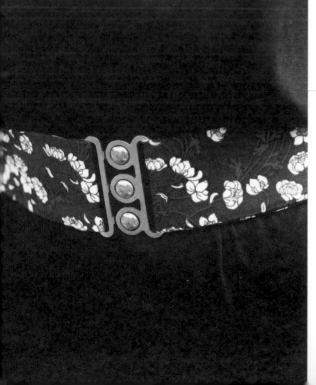

5 Fold the two fabric strips right sides together. Taking ⅜-in (1-cm) seam allowances, and reversing at each end, sew along the pressed fold at the top from either end of the zipper to the ends of the strips. Sew as close to the ends of the zipper as you can, so that there won't be any holes in your pocket. Then sew right along the bottom edge.

UNDER CANVAS...

6 Turn the belt right side out through one of the open short ends and press it flat. Tuck in ⅜in (1cm) at each short end and press.

7 Slip one short end through one half of the clasp and sew it to the inside layer of the belt. Repeat on the other end with the other half of the clasp. It you are using a buckle, attach it to one end of the belt in this way, and follow the instructions of the eyelet kit to fit eyelets into the other end of the belt.

8 To make the pocket, stick strips of masking tape across the belt just beyond either end of the zipper. Sew along these guidelines, reversing at each end to secure the stitching.

Serious

SNUGGLE POWER

YOU'RE GOING TO NEED...

- Hot water bottle: mine is 13 x 8in (33 x 20cm) and this case is quite a loose fit (as I find that easiest to use), so adjust the measurements to suit your own bottle
- Pieces of fleece measuring 10 x 15¼in (25 x 39cm) and 10 x 3in (25 x 8cm)
- Piece of fur fabric measuring 10 x 13in (25 x 33cm)
- 10in (25cm) zipper
- Pins
- Hand-sewing needle
- Basting thread: I always use ordinary sewing thread in a contrast color
- Fabric scissors
- Sewing threads to match fabrics
- Sewing machine
- Pom-pom trim (optional)

Long before glamping was a thing, Lovely Clare camped in style. That kettle of water boiled at bedtime wasn't for tea, it was for Lovely Clare's hot water bottle. I had never thought to bring a hottie camping, imagining that shivering was just part of the experience. Now I know better and have perfected the camping hottie cover, shared with you here. It's quick and easy to make, the fur-and-fleece combo is seriously snuggly in a chilly tent, the zipper has fleece on both sides so it doesn't get caught in the fur, and the whole thing is washable and quick drying.

1 Lay the zipper face down on the right side of the large piece of fleece with one tape aligned with a 10in (25cm) edge. Pin and then baste the tape in place. (I always prefer to baste zippers as I find it quicker and easier than sewing a pinned zipper and then taking out all the wobbly stitches and starting again.)

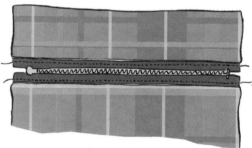

2 Baste the other zipper tape to the right side of the smaller piece of fleece in the same way. Using a zipper foot, machine-sew the zipper to each piece of fleece, stitching close to the teeth. Take out the basting stitches. Fold both pieces of fabric along the stitching line away from the zipper and press flat.

3 | Trim about ⅜in (1cm) of the top fur away from the base fabric (basically, give the fur a haircut) all around the edges—you don't need to be precise, but try not to trim more than that or some bald patches might appear. Lay the fleece/zipper combo right side down on the fur, matching the edge of the small piece of fleece with the fabric edge of the furry piece. Taking a ⅜-in (1-cm) seam allowance, sew the seam.

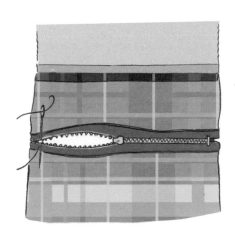

4 | At one end of the zipper, pinch the ends of the tapes together so that they stick up on the wrong side and whip stitch (see page 133) them together. Sew the tapes at the other end in the same way. Open the zipper halfway: this is essential!

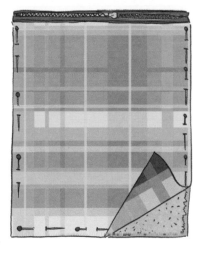

5 | Fold the joined fabrics right sides together with the zipper at the top and pin them all around. Taking a ⅜-in (1-cm) seam allowance, sew around all three open sides, reversing at each end to secure the stitching. Turn right side out through the opened zipper (that's why opening it was essential).

6 | You can add an embellishment to the zipper pull, but nothing spiky that'll prick your toes in the night. And that's it, your snuggle cover is done.

Wrap UP WARM

YOU'RE GOING TO NEED...

- 1⅔yd (1.5m) each of 55-in (140-cm) wide main fabric and lining fabric: I used needlecord for the main fabric and brushed cotton for the lining
- Pieces of fabric measuring 16½ x 2in (42 x 5cm) and 16½ x 12in (42 x 30cm) for the pocket: I used needlecord
- 14in (35cm) zipper
- Fabric scissors
- Pins
- Sewing threads to match fabrics
- Sewing machine
- Hand-sewing needle
- Basting thread: I always use ordinary sewing thread in a contrast color
- Iron and ironing board
- Charm for zipper pull (optional)
- Piece of strong, medium-weight cotton fabric, 17¼ x 14in (44 x 35cm) with pinked edges

INSIDE OUT?

The wrap is reversible, but I've called one side the "lining" and the other the "main fabric" just for ease in the instructions. Obviously, worn one way around the pocket will be on the outside.

Keeping cozy is a camper's challenge, so here's an easy-to-make hooded, giant wrap that'll keep you both warm and looking lovely; not a common combination in camping gear. And there's a practical pocket so you don't need to carry a bag if you're wandering a festival site. I've gone for warm but lightweight fabrics, but you could make a super-snug version in fleece or machine-washable wool (important to be practical here).

1 Square off both ends of the main and lining fabrics. Cut a 12in (30cm) strip off both pieces and set aside for the hood. Cut the selvages off the rest of both pieces of fabric, then cut them in half lengthwise, to give two pieces about 27½ x 47in (70 x 120cm). Taking a ⅜-in (1-cm) seam allowance, join the short ends of the two main pieces to make a strip about 94in (2.4m) long by 27½in (70cm) wide (precise measurements don't matter, as long as your wrap is as giant as you want it to be, and the seam is in the middle). Join the lining pieces in the same way and trim the lining to fit the main fabric if need be. Press the seams open. Set aside.

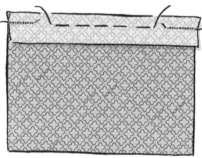

MAKING THE POCKET

2 Press under a ⅜in (1cm) hem along one long edge of both pocket pieces. Open out the edges again and place the two pieces right sides together, matching the pressed lines. Sew up 1½in (4cm) of the seam at each end. Baste along the rest of the seam.

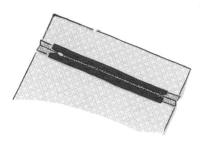

3 | Lay the pocket flat and face down. Position the zipper right side down on the basted opening, with the teeth over the basting and the tape ends running onto the seam allowances of the stitched sections of the seam. Pin and then baste the zipper in place along the tapes.

4 | Fit a zipper foot on the sewing machine and machine-sew the zipper in place, sewing as close to the teeth as possible.

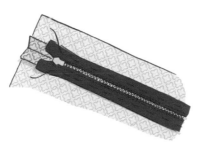

5 | Unpick the basting stitches from the right side. You can add a charm to the zipper pull if you want (and I did want).

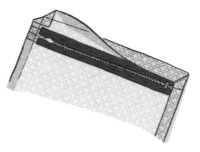

6 |

Press under a ⅝-in (1.5-cm) hem all around the pocket. At the corners, make miters by pressing under a triangle where the pressed lines cross, then folding the hems back in and pressing everything flat.

WRAP UP WARM

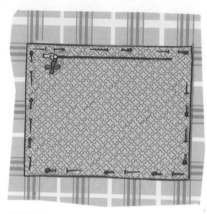

8 Turn the lining over and, using the pins as guides, pin the piece of strong cotton fabric over the back of the pocket: this will reinforce the pocket seams and help prevent the lining tearing when you put things in the pocket. Turn the lining over again and re-pin the pocket from the right side, making sure you pin on the backing cotton. Then take out the pins put in from the wrong side. Topstitch the pocket in place right around the edges.

7 Position the pocket on the right side of the lining where you want it to be: mine is quite low down on what will be the left-hand side of the wrap. Pin it in place around the edges.

9 Cut the pieces set aside for the hood to measure 31½ x 12in (80 x 30cm). Fold each in half lengthwise and, taking a ⅜in (1cm) seam allowance, sew one long seam. Snip off the corner of the seam allowance at the fold.

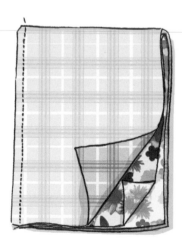

10 Turn the main piece right side out—pushing out the corner neatly—and leave the lining piece wrong side out. Slip the main piece into the lining, matching the seams and raw edges, and pin then machine-sew them together around the long raw edge, taking a ⅜-in (1-cm) seam allowance.

11 Turn the main fabric wrong side out and hand-sew the seam allowances together at the folded corner.

12 Turn the hood right side out, tucking the lining into the main fabric, and press the front edge. Zigzag stitch the layers together along the bottom raw edge.

13 Right sides together, pin the hood to the wrap main fabric, matching the wrap center seam with the hood back seam. Machine-sew them together, taking a ¼-in (6-mm) seam allowance.

MAKING UP THE WRAP

14 Right sides together, lay the lining over the main fabric (and hood), matching the raw edges. Taking a ⅜-in (1-cm) seam allowance, sew the pieces together all around, leaving a 6in (15cm) gap. Clip off the seam allowances at the corners, about ⅛in (3mm) from the stitching. Turn the wrap right side out through the gap and press the wrap flat all around, pressing under the seam allowances at the gap.

15 Topstitch right around the wrap, hood included, stitching ⅛in (3mm) in from the edge.

Today
I'M WEARING...

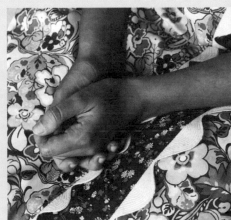

TRICK

Hats are a thing. They are everywhere, and there's a style for everyone; you just need to find the perfect one for you. And as well as being on-trend, they are so useful: Bad hair day? Who, me? Nooooo, just loving my hat… But gorgeous hats can be expensive: you know the answer—buy an inexpensive plain one and decorate it yourself. It's very quick and simple to do.

YOU'RE GOING TO NEED...

- 33½in (85cm) of ¼-in (6-mm) wide stiff ribbon
- Sewing thread to match ribbons
- Hand-sewing needle
- 1¼in (3-cm) diameter four-hole button: I used a vintage mother-of-pearl one
- Some feathers: I used one down feather and two smooth ones
- 13in (33cm) of 2-in (5-cm) wide velvet ribbon
- ¾-in (2-cm) diameter decorative button: I used a vintage green plastic one
- Embroidery floss
- Long embroidery needle
- Hat of your choice

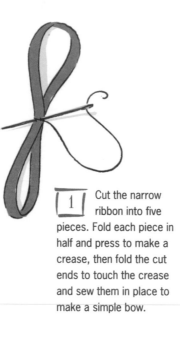

1 Cut the narrow ribbon into five pieces. Fold each piece in half and press to make a crease, then fold the cut ends to touch the crease and sew them in place to make a simple bow.

2 Make five bows in total and stack them on top of one another, as shown. Sew them together firmly to make a flower-like piece.

3 Using sewing thread, sew the large button to the center of the ribbon flower. Sew in a square shape through the four holes to attach the flower evenly to the back of the button.

TODAY I'M WEARING...

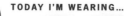

4 Make a mini-posy of feathers and bind and sew it together, using a sharp needle to sew through the quills to stop the feathers shifting.

5 Sew the feather posy to the back of the ribbon flower. Trim the ends of the quills.

6 Fold under and sew a narrow hem on both ends of the velvet ribbon and sew them in. Then work a row of small running stitches along one edge of the ribbon, pulling them up to gather the edge.

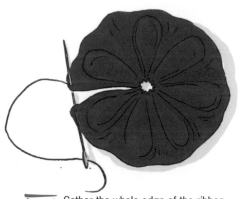

7 Gather the whole edge of the ribbon, then pull the gathers as tight as possible and fasten off the thread. Sew the hemmed ends together to make a rosette.

8 Sewing through the holes in the button as in Step 3, sew the rosette to the back of the button/flower/feather posy, arranging the feathers to cover the join in the rosette.

9 If you want/need to, change the ribbon around the crown of the hat now: I chose a velvet ribbon that toned with my rosette. Thread a long embroidery needle with floss and knot one end, leaving a 4in (10cm) tail. From inside the hat, push the needle through where you want to attach the rosette. Push the needle through the rosette to emerge from a hole in the big button, then thread on the decorative button and take the needle back through the big button and rosette, and back into the hat. Make a second stitch through all the elements, then tie the ends of floss firmly together inside the hat.

Pearly
PETER PAN

Little House on the Prairie meets a London Pearly Queen: wear it over a sweater or boat-neck top as a collar, or with a sundress as a festival necklace (it's quick to make, so if it ends up covered in mud, you can just wash it, or cut off the buttons and start again). Alternatively, make your version from black velvet with vintage jet and silver buttons for gothic bling, or go for a button-box-raid look with a heavy sprinkling of buttons of all shapes, sizes, and colors on a collar of candy-stripe cotton, or... There are as many options as there are buttons and fabrics: that's a lot of options.

YOU'RE GOING TO NEED...
- Collar template on page 142
- Sheet of newspaper
- Paper scissors and fabric scissors
- Two pieces of fabric and one piece of medium-weight fusible interfacing, each measuring 13 x 20½in (33 x 52cm): I used linen fabric
- Iron and ironing board
- Pins
- 1yd (1m) of ⅝-in (1.5-mm) wide tape or ribbon: I used linen tape
- Basting thread and sewing thread to match fabric and trim
- Hand-sewing needle
- Sewing machine
- 37½in (95cm) of narrow trim: I used a small daisy trim
- Selection of buttons: I used vintage mother-of-pearl
- Six-strand embroidery floss
- Embroidery needle

1 Enlarge the template by 200 percent. To make a muslin, fold the newspaper in half, place the center back of the template on the fold and cut out a paper collar. Cut off ⅜in (1cm) all around (you don't have to measure this perfectly, a rough cut will do). Try on this paper muslin to make sure the collar will be the right size for you. If need be, adjust the paper muslin to fit and make a bespoke pattern, remembering to add the seam allowances back on. Cut out two fabric collars and one from interfacing. Iron the interfacing onto one fabric piece, then trim off ⅛in (3mm) all around the outer edge; this piece will be the undercollar.

2 Cut the tape in half. Pin one end of each half to the front edge of the right side of the undercollar, ½in (12mm) from the inside neck edge, as shown. Make sure the ends of the tapes are square to the edges of the collar, then baste them in place.

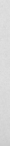

84 TODAY I'M WEARING...

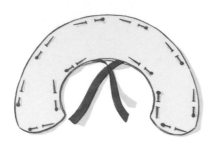

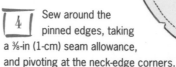

3 | Lay the other fabric piece right-side down on top of the undercollar and pin the pieces together around the edges. Leave a 4in (10cm) gap in the center back neck, and pull the ends of the tape through the gap so that you can see them.

4 | Sew around the pinned edges, taking a ⅜-in (1-cm) seam allowance, and pivoting at the neck-edge corners. Be very careful not to catch the tapes in the stitching. Clip notches in the seam allowances, clipping to within ⅛in (3mm) of the line of stitching. Make notches close together on tightly curved or short sections, and space them more widely on gentle, longer curves.

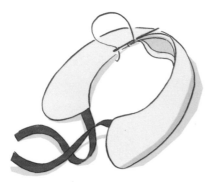

5 | Turn the collar right side out through the gap. Press the seams, rolling them to the undercollar side as you go, and press under the seam allowances across the gap. Ladder stitch (see page 134) the gap closed.

6 | Hand-sew the trim around the edge of the collar. Make tiny stitches in matching thread through the trim, and through the upper layer only of the collar, to sew it on as invisibly as possible.

7 | Arrange buttons on each end of the collar (or all around it if you prefer) and take digital photos. Sew on the buttons one at a time, using your photos as guides. Use one, two, or three strands of six-strand floss, as appropriate for the size of the button. You can use decorative stitches, such as fly stitch: bring the needle and floss out through one hole in the button and down through another, leaving a loose loop of floss. Then bring the needle up though the fabric at the edge of the button, and through the loop of floss. Make a short straight stitch to anchor the loop and complete the fly stitch. Four fly stitches on a four-hole button will make a star; two stitches on a two-hole button will make a diamond.

8 | Or you can use chain stitch: bring the needle and floss out through one hole in the button and down through the same hole, leaving a loose loop of floss. Then bring the needle up through the fabric at the edge of the button, and through the loop of floss. Make a short straight stitch to anchor the loop and complete the chain stitch. You can work a line of three chain stitches across a two-hole button (the middle stitch will span the holes). You can also work straight stitches in squares or crosses on four-hole buttons.

Big

BOW

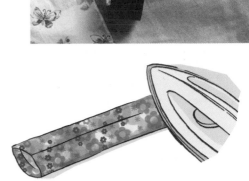

Here's a perky hair bow that you can make from just a few scraps of fabric, to match a dress you've made maybe? And it's not just a project for little girls; big girls look good with bows, too. Though if you aren't the bow type, you can just stop at Step 4 and make a simple, but chic, hairband.

YOU'RE GOING TO NEED...

- For the band: strip of fabric and strip of lightweight fusible interfacing, each measuring 3in (8cm) shorter than the circumference of your head where you want the band to sit, by 4¾in (12cm)
- 4in (10cm) of 1¼-in (3-cm) wide elastic
- For the bow: two pieces of fabric measuring 9½ x 8in (24 x 20cm) and one piece measuring 3½ x 2¾in (9 x 7cm)
- Fabric scissors
- Iron and ironing board
- Pins
- Sewing threads to match fabrics
- Sewing machine
- Hand-sewing needle

1 Iron the interfacing onto the back of the band piece of fabric. Right side in, fold the fabric in half lengthwise and, taking a ⅜-in (1-cm) seam allowance, sew the long seam. Fold back one seam allowance and press open, without pressing a fold in the tube of fabric.

2 Turn the tube right side out. Roll the seam to center back and press the tube flat. Tuck in ⅜in (1cm) at each end and press flat.

3 Push ⅜in (1cm) of elastic into one end of the tube. On the back, fold the corners of the fabric in, as shown, and pin to hold the folds.

4 Sewing either by hand or machine, sew back and forth across the fabric a couple of times. Sew the other end of elastic into the other end of the tube to make a hairband. Check that the hairband isn't twisted before you sew. The folded layers of fabric plus the elastic are quite thick, so use a thimble to help you push the needle through if you're hand-sewing, and sew slowly if you're using a machine.

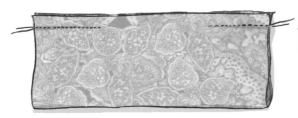

5 Right side in, fold one of the large bow pieces in half lengthwise. From each end and taking a ⅜-in (1-cm) seam allowance, sew a short length of the seam, so that there is a 2-in (5-cm) gap in the middle.

6 Roll the seam to center back and press the tube flat, pressing the seam allowances open. Taking the same seam allowance, sew across the short ends, then cut off the corners within the seam allowances. Turn right side out, pushing out the corners neatly, and press. Make up the second large bow piece the same way, but fold it in half widthwise.

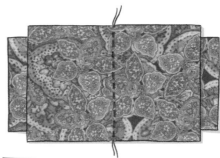

7 Stack the shorter, wider piece on top of the longer thinner one, centering them. Using doubled sewing thread, stitch a line of short gathering stitches across the middle of the bow-to-be, sewing through all layers.

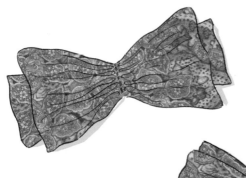

8 Pull the gathers up as tightly as possible to make a bow. Secure the thread by stitching back and forth a few times through the gathered section.

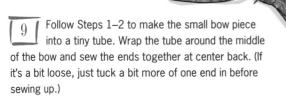

9 Follow Steps 1–2 to make the small bow piece into a tiny tube. Wrap the tube around the middle of the bow and sew the ends together at center back. (If it's a bit loose, just tuck a bit more of one end in before sewing up.)

10 Sewing through the back of the bow center, sew the bow to the hairband. I've sewn mine on at a jaunty angle, but you could go Minnie Mouse-style and perch your bow right on top.

Pretty

+PRACTICAL+PERFECT

An apron is a cooking necessity (especially if you are a cook as enthusiastic but messy as I am), but to be a hostess with the mostest, it needs to be lovely as well as capacious; so that you can pop in and out of the kitchen and join in the party without constantly taking your apron off, forgetting to put it back on again, and spilling cooking ingredients down your front. I like a longish apron as I wear a lot of long skirts, but you can easily adapt this pattern to suit both the length you like and your waist size—see Size Matters, below, and the **CHANGE THIS** notes in the steps.

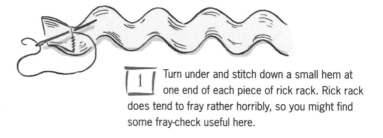

1 Turn under and stitch down a small hem at one end of each piece of rick rack. Rick rack does tend to fray rather horribly, so you might find some fray-check useful here.

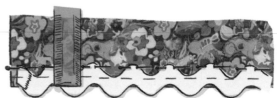

2 Right sides together, lay the jumbo rick rack along the left-hand long edge of the large piece of main fabric, with the turned under end ⅜in (1cm) up from a short raw edge. Position the rick rack so that when a ⅝in (1.5cm) seam is sewn along the long edge, the seam will run along the middle of the rick rack: shown here by the dashed line. Pin the rick rack in place along the upper edge.

3 | Lay the contrast strip for the skirt right side down over the rick rack, matching the raw edges with the raw edges of the main piece. Pin the layers together, making sure you pin through the rick rack, then take out the pins inserted in Step 2. Sew the seam taking a ⅝-in (1.5-cm) seam allowance. Finish the raw seam allowances by zigzag stitching them and the rick rack together.

4 | Press the seam flat on the right side, pressing the rick rack toward the contrast strip, and on the wrong side pressing the rick rack and both seam allowances toward the main fabric.

5 | Repeat Steps 2–4 with the super-jumbo rick rack, pinning it right sides together to the raw edge of the contrast strip, then pinning the smaller piece of main fabric over it. Press the rick rack and seam allowances in the same direction as the first piece. On the right side, topstitch ⅛in (3mm) from the rick rack seams to hold the seam allowances flat.

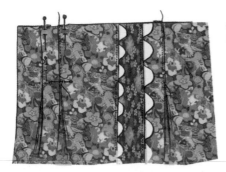

6 | Pleat the top edge of the apron. I made three pleats, each over 2¼in (6cm) of fabric, placing one pleat 2½in (6.5cm) in from each edge and another one in the larger main fabric, 1½in (4cm) from the first pleat. You can **CHANGE THIS** arrangement to suit, but keep the pleats at least 1¼in (3cm) from the long edges, and don't put a pleat into the contrast strip (it'll get muddled up in the rick rack seams and be very bulky). On the right side, topstitch a short way down the pleats to hold them in place: I topstitched about 4in (10cm), but you can **CHANGE THIS** by stitching a shorter amount for a fuller apron. At this stage my apron was 16½in (42cm) wide across the top edge.

7 | Turn under and sew a double ⅜-in (1-cm) hem along each long edge. This made the top edge of my apron a finished width of 15in (38cm).

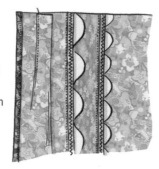

8 | Iron the fusible interfacing onto the back of half of the waistband fabric, as shown. Right sides together, pin one tie piece to each end of the waistband. Taking ⅝-in (1.5-cm) seam allowances, sew the pieces together. Press the seam allowances open.

9 Right sides together, pin the interfaced edge of the waistband to the top of the skirt, matching the waistband side seams to the edges of the skirt. Sew the pieces together, taking a ⅜-in (1-cm) seam allowance.

10 Open the pieces out and press the seam flat, pressing the seam allowance toward the waistband. Press under ⅜-in (1-cm) hems around all the other edges of the waistband/tie piece.

11 Fold the piece in half along the interfacing and matching the edges of the ties exactly, and sew all around.

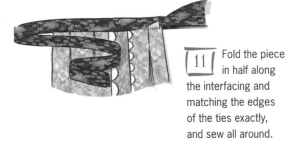

12 Open out one folded edge of the bias binding and, right sides together, pin it to the bottom edge of the apron, matching the edge of the binding to the edge of the apron as shown, and so that ⅜in (1cm) protrudes at either side. Sew along the fold in the binding.

13 Fold in the free ends of the binding and press. Then fold the binding over to the wrong side of the apron, folding over just a little of the fabric as well, as shown. Sew along the top edge of the binding to finish the hem. I stopped and started sewing either side of the rick rack, but that isn't strictly necessary.

Patchwork
POOCH

- Diagram on page 140
- Piece of backing fabric the size of the coat: see Customizing the Pattern, below
- Tape measure, pencil, and ruler
- Scraps of fabric for patchwork
- Fabric scissors
- Hand-sewing needle
- Basting thread: I always use ordinary sewing thread in a contrast color
- Pins
- Sewing threads to match fabrics
- Sewing machine
- Iron and ironing board
- Scraps of trimming and iron-on patches
- Enough ¾-in (2-cm) wide bias binding to go right around the circumference of the coat
- Two snap fastenings

CUSTOMIZING THE PATTERN

On the diagram on page 140 there are arrows telling you which bits of your dog to measure so that you can draw out your own pattern to fit. I advise cutting a coat from newspaper first and making sure it will fit before starting work on the fabric.

Your dog is bound to vary in size and shape to my Elvis, but this is a simple coat pattern that can be adjusted to suit any size of pooch. And while I've gone for a simplified version of crazy patchwork that's doable for novice sewcalists, you can use as many fabrics as you want, and add as many embellishments as you want to make your dog a coat of many colors.

1 Using a pencil and ruler, draw out the pattern on the backing fabric. You can draw around the base of a mug or small plate (depending on the scale of your coat) to create the curves. Cut it out roughly, leaving about ¾in (2cm) all around.

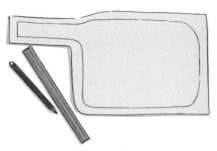

MAKING THE PATCHWORK

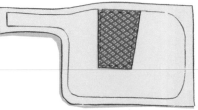

2 Cut the first patch from fabric, making it about half the width of the coat. Pin then baste it to the backing, matching one edge to the drawn edge of the coat. (I always baste the first patch as I find it makes life easier, but I don't baste any others.)

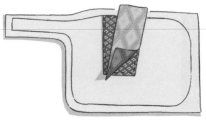

3 Cut a second patch that's a bit longer than the first one. Lay it right side down on the first patch, matching one side edge and with some fabric overlapping at each end.

TODAY I'M WEARING...

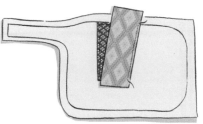

4 Sew the patches to the backing fabric, taking a ⅜-in (1-cm) seam allowance.

5 Fold the second patch out flat and press. Use the pencil and ruler to mark off the edges of the second patch to align with the first, then cut off the excess fabric.

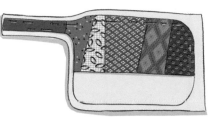

6 Continue in this way to cover one half of the coat with patched fabric, including the chest strap. Pin the patches in place around the outer edges. Remove the basting stitches.

7 Taking ⅜-in (1-cm) seam allowances, piece together some fabrics to make a strip wide enough to cover the other half of the coat. Press all the seam allowances open.

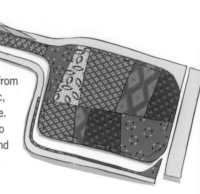

8 Pin then sew the strip to the top section of the coat in the same way as for the previous patches. You can offset the seam a bit so that it won't run in a straight line down the dog's spine. Press the strip flat onto the backing and pin it around the outer edges.

9 Cut out the coat from the backing fabric, following your drawn edge. Set the sewing machine to a medium zigzag stitch and sew all around the edges, sewing all the patches to the backing.

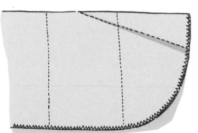

MAKING THE COAT

10 At this stage, try the coat on your dog, safety pinning the chest strap closed. If your hound has a roundish derrière—as Elvis does—then you might want to put a dart in to improve fit. I've made a dart that's 1¼in (3cm) wide at the base and 4¾in (12cm) long. Press the dart to

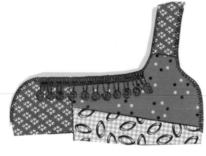

11 You can add some trimmings: I've chosen a little pom-pom trim around the neckline. Just baste it on at this stage.

12 Iron the bias binding in half along its length. Fold in and iron ⅜in (1cm) at one end. Starting halfway along the top of the chest strap, slip the folded binding over the edge of the fabric. Topstitch the binding in place, sewing ⅛in (3mm) in from the folded binding edge, to the end of the strap.

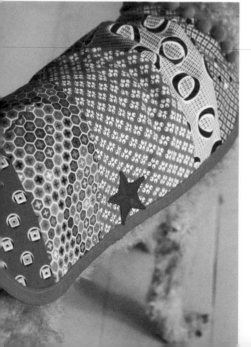

TODAY I'M WEARING...

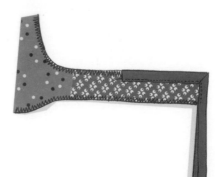

13 Miter the binding at a right angle across the end of the strap and sew in place. Miter it again and sew the binding on down the other side of the strap and continue around the rest of the coat.

14 At the curved end of the coat, I found it best to stop machine sewing and baste the binding around the curves, using lots of steam from the iron and stretching the folded edge with my fingers to make a neat curve. Once it's basted in place, topstitch as before.

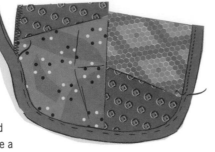

15 At the back neck the binding covers the band of the pom-pom trim neatly. When you get close to the starting point, trim the binding ⅜in (1cm) longer than needed, fold in the end, butt it up to the starting point, and topstitch over it.

16 Cut a strip of fabric long enough to be a tummy strap and twice as wide as needed plus ¾in (2cm). Follow Steps 1–2 of Big Bow (see page 87) to make a tube with tucked-in ends.

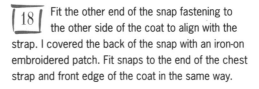

17 Try the coat on your dog again and pin the tummy strap in position on the inside of the coat, being careful not to stab the pooch with the pin. Sew the strap on with firm whip stitches (see page 133), sewing through the lining only. Fix a snap fastening to the other end of the strap.

18 Fit the other end of the snap fastening to the other side of the coat to align with the strap. I covered the back of the snap with an iron-on embroidered patch. Fit snaps to the end of the chest strap and front edge of the coat in the same way.

Big

BELT

- Two pieces of fabric cut to your waist measurement (but you may wish to make them 2in (5cm) longer for comfort—you can then overlap the ends if needed when the belt is worn), by a width you feel comfortable wearing, plus ⅜-in (1-cm) seam allowances all around: my fabric is 5½in (14cm) wide for a finished belt 4¾in (12cm) wide
- One piece of heavyweight fusible interfacing the same size as the fabric
- Fabric scissors
- Iron and ironing board
- Fading fabric marker
- Pins
- Sewing threads to match fabric and ribbon
- Sewing machine
- Hand-sewing needle
- Point turner or butter knife
- Tassel or charm (optional)
- 3yd (3m) of ⅝-in (1.5-cm) wide ribbon
- Basting thread: I always use ordinary sewing thread in a contrast color

A version of a Japanese obi belt, this is a very quick project to make, and ideal for using up smallish pieces of fabric left over from dressmaking projects. Made a dress with contrast cuffs and collar? Make a big belt to coordinate with it. The tassel I've added is a nod to the traditional netsuke worn with obi belts; you can add any charm or decoration you like, or none at all.

1 Iron the fusible interfacing onto the back of the fabric that will be the right side of the belt. Using the fabric marker, round off the corners, as shown (I drew around the edge of my coffee cup).

2 Place the pieces of fabric right sides together and pin. Taking a ⅜-in (1-cm) seam allowance, machine-sew right around the belt, following the drawn lines at the corners and leaving a 4-in (10-cm) gap in one long edge. Take out the pins. Clip notches in the seam allowances around the curves, spacing them about ¼in (6mm) apart and cutting to within ⅛in (3mm) of the stitching. Trim all the seam allowances to ¼in (6mm), other than across the open gap.

3 Turn the belt right side out through the gap, carefully pushing out the corners to be smoothly rounded (a butter knife is useful here if you don't have a bespoke point turner). Ladder stitch (see page 134) the gap closed.

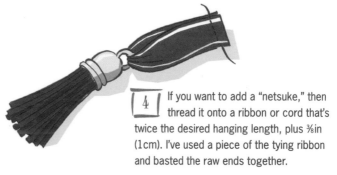

4 If you want to add a "netsuke," then thread it onto a ribbon or cord that's twice the desired hanging length, plus ⅜in (1cm). I've used a piece of the tying ribbon and basted the raw ends together.

5 Pin the ribbon to the right side of the belt, centering it top to bottom and with an equal amount free at each end for tying. Tuck ⅜in (1cm) of the hanging loop of the netsuke under the edge of the ribbon: I placed mine a little to one side of the middle of the belt so that it will hang to one side when the belt is worn. Starting 4in (10cm) from one end of the belt, baste the ribbon in place, sewing right along to the other end of the belt. Remove the pins.

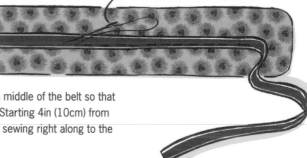

6 Using thread to match the ribbon, and sewing very slowly and carefully, machine-sew along the lower edge of the ribbon, stitching right on the edge. Follow the basting, so that the stitching starts 4in (10cm) from one end of the belt and continues right along to the other end. Repeat along the top edge.

7 To wear the belt, wrap it around your waist with the ends at the back, tucking the free end under the ribboned end if the ends do not meet exactly, then wrap the ribbons around to the front and tie them in a bow. You can trim the ends of the ribbon if need be.

STITCHING ON THE EDGE

It does take a bit of practice to edge-stitch beautifully, and the best way to master the technique is on lined paper. Slip the paper under the foot, then turn the sewing machine hand wheel to lower the needle until it is touching a line on the paper. Note the position of the toes of the foot in relation to the line. Sew along the line, watching the position of the toes rather than the up-and-down movement of the needle, as that will be distracting. Most sewing machines allow you to move the needle position left to right, so you can align the line on the paper with the edge of a toe of the foot, then move the needle until it is on the line. Sew as many straight lines as you need to to feel comfortable with the technique, then change the needle (sewing paper will blunt it), and sew on the ribbon.

Blooming
MARVELOUS

YOU'RE GOING TO NEED...
- Two pieces of man-made fiber organza, a bit larger than you want the flower to be
- Fabric scissors
- Candle
- Sewing thread to match fabric
- Hand-sewing needle
- Decorative buttons and beads
- Hairclip finding

Exuberant, easy to make, inexpensive, endlessly customizable, infinitely wearable, and they will never fade or need watering: what more could a girl want from a flower? I've attached these orange blooms to hairclips, but you can sew them to a brooch finding, a hairband (see page 87), a wrist strap for a corsage... simply anywhere a flower is needed. You need to be a little bit careful using the candle, and this certainly isn't a project for children to make on their own, but once the edges of the petals have been singed, the flowers come together quickly and easily.

1 Cut the pieces of organza into rough circles (they really don't have to be very round), one slightly smaller than the other, and cut four slits in the edge, as shown.

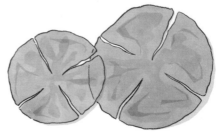

2 Hold the edge of the organza close to a candle flame and you'll see it start to curl up and create rounded edges to the slits, forming petals. You want to achieve a curled edge that isn't actually burnt, so experiment with positioning the fabric to get the right result.

3 Stack the petals on top of one another. Using doubled matching thread, sew a small circle of running stitches into the middle of the stack, through both layers.

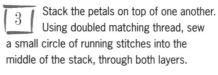

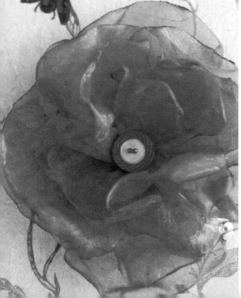

TODAY I'M WEARING...

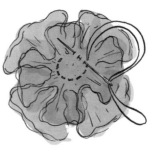

4 | Pull the gathers up as tightly as possible and secure the thread on the back.

5 | Sew a decorative button or two into the middle of the flower: I've stacked two buttons and threaded on a couple of beads as well.

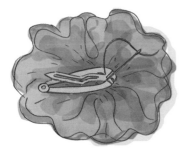

6 | Sew the little puff of fabric on the back (created by making the gathers in Step 4) to a hairclip finding, or whatever else you choose.

Button-on
BROOCH

Wear your heart on your sleeve—or at least on your jacket—with this seriously simple-to-make button-on brooch. The slit in the template fits over a ⅝in (1.5cm) diameter button, so if you have a different size button, make the slit larger or smaller accordingly (you can test it on a scrap of felt before embroidering your brooch). You can adapt the idea to make different shapes: a flower brooch over a plain colored button would be lovely, or a leaf shape with a ladybug button, or a randomly curved shape over a geometric button…

YOU'RE GOING TO NEED...

- Heart template on page 138
- Piece of felt, measuring at least 4in (10cm) square
- Piece of medium-weight fusible interfacing, measuring at least 4in (10cm) square
- Iron and ironing board
- Fading fabric marker
- Small, sharp embroidery scissors
- Machine embroidery threads: I used a variegated thread and a plain one
- Sewing machine with free-motion embroidery foot

MACHINE EMBROIDERY

This is a great project if you haven't done any machine embroidery before, as you can pretty much just scribble away to your heart's content. It would be best to practice a bit on scrap fabric, just to get the feel of moving the fabric around under the needle.

Because the feed dogs are lowered, they aren't feeding the fabric through under the needle, so you need to move the fabric yourself. This is a small piece of fairly firm fabric, so a hoop isn't needed, but do be careful to keep your fingers away from the needle.

You might need to fiddle with the tension setting on your machine to get it right for embroidery.

Don't be tempted to sew very slowly; it's actually easier to embroider with a bit of speed. You're aiming to move the fabric smoothly under the needle, drawing with the resulting stitches.

1 Iron the fusible interfacing onto the back of the felt. Using the fabric marker, draw around the template on the felt and mark the slit.

2 Start by embroidering around the slit; go over the line a couple of times to create a firm edge. Then embroider a line around the outside edge of the heart.

TODAY I'M WEARING...

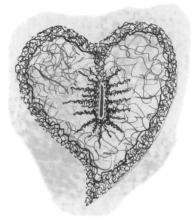

3 Next, fill in the heart with scribbles, going around and around in circles. I used a variegated thread for this to give color changes. Then make a border of tighter scribbles around the outside edges in plain thread.

4 Using small, sharp scissors, cut out the heart and cut open the slit. It doesn't matter if you snip a few threads; the dense stitching won't unravel much.

Patched
UP

In my school's 1970s production of *Joseph and the Amazing Technicolor Dreamcoat*, the eponymous garment was a denim jean jacket covered in embroidered patches, lovingly stitched on by Mrs Chewins, proud mother of Joseph, aka Max. As a lowly member of the Egyptian chorus (and one asked to mime rather than actually sing, as my tone-deaf vocals put off those around me), I was deeply, deeply jealous of that jacket. So I'm thrilled that the "goes around, comes around" nature of fashion has brought us these patches once again (and jean jackets have never really gone away). My patches let you use up the tiniest scraps of gorgeous printed fabrics, and they look brilliant mixed in with purchased embroidered patches, too.

1 Iron a piece of fusible interfacing onto the back of the piece of fabric you want to use. On the right side, draw out the shape of the patch. Don't make very tight curves as they'll be difficult to satin stitch neatly around.

2 Set the sewing machine to satin stitch: a very tight, medium-width zigzag stitch. You might want to experiment with this on spare bits of fabric if it's new to you. Satin stitch around the drawn line. If you need to pivot the fabric, stop sewing with the needle down on the outer edge of the stitching; that will help keep the outline of the patch smooth.

TODAY I'M WEARING...

3 Very carefully cut out the shape around the edge of the stitching, being sure not to cut through any stitches. For a super-neat finish, work another ring of satin stitch over the first one, so that the stitches overlap the cut edge and cover any trace of fabric there. But this really is optional.

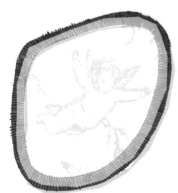

4 Lay the patch face down on a scrap of fusible webbing and draw around it with a pencil. Cut out the shape just inside the drawn line. Place the webbing right side down on the back of the patch, check that it overlaps the stitching (tuck the ends of thread under it to secure them), and trim any bits that protrude, then iron the webbing in place.

5 To attach the patch to a jacket (or anything else), peel off the paper backing and iron it in place. You can add a few stitches, sewing over the satin stitches, if need be.

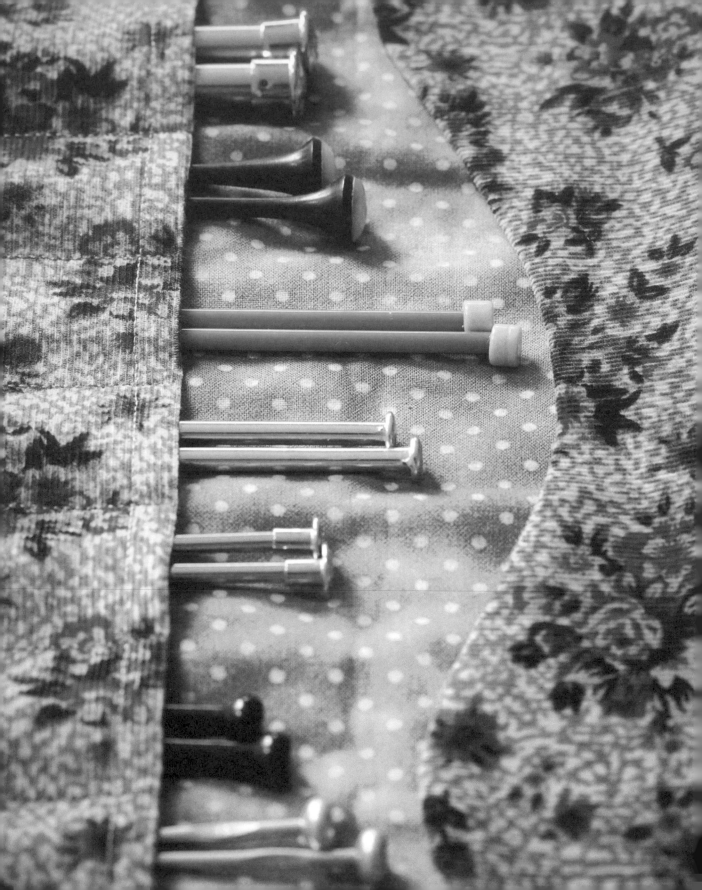

CHAPTER 4

I like
TO MAKE...

Knitter's

BUCKET BAG

YOU'RE GOING TO NEED...

- Piece of thick fabric measuring 5 x 10¼in (13 x 26cm), for knitting needle pocket: you can make this wider to hold more sets of needles if you want
- One piece of furnishing-weight fabric measuring 23 x 16in (58 x 40cm), for the body of the bag, and one measuring 16½ x 4½in (42 x 11cm), for the handle: this was the length I liked, you can adjust it to suit you
- Circle of thick fabric, 8in (20cm) in diameter: I used a chenille furnishing fabric
- Circle of cotton fabric, 8in (20cm) in diameter and piece measuring 23 x 16in (58 x 40cm), for the lining
- Small pieces of fabric for inside pocket/s: make as many as you want at whatever sizes you want
- Piece of ribbon for safety-pin loop
- Fabric scissors
- Iron and ironing board
- Pins
- Sewing threads to match fabrics
- Sewing machine
- Masking tape
- Hand-sewing needle

This is the perfect project bag: seriously. It's deep enough to hold lots of balls of yarn, but not huge and unwieldy. It's got a flat bottom so it will stand up, and a handle you can make whichever length you like for a bag. It has pockets for knitting needles and other kit, and a loop for dropped-stitch-emergency safety pins and stitch holders. And it's good-looking, and quick and easy to make in your favorite colors: or if you are super-geek coordinated, in colors to match your knitting project...

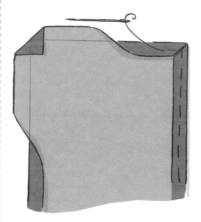

1 Start by making the needle pocket. If your fabric will fray, zigzag or serge the edges (mine didn't fray). Press under a ⅜in (1cm) hem all around. At the corners, fold over the point at the pressed lines, then fold in the hems to make a neat miter; baste the hems and miters in place.

2 Sew the top hem of the pocket piece and fasten off the threads on the back. Lay the bag body fabric flat and right side up, with the long edges at the top and bottom. Pin the pocket in position: you can place it wherever you like, mine is pretty much centered. Topstitching ¼in (6mm) in from the edges, sew around three sides of the pocket, reversing at the top corners for strength. Fasten off the threads on the back.

3 Use masking tape to mark out the lines of stitching that will divide the pocket: I've measured ¾in (2cm) in from each side, so the middle section will be wider, to hold thicker needles. Sew along the outside edge of each piece of tape, reversing at the top for strength. Fasten off the threads on the back.

4 Fold the bag piece in half and, taking a ⅜-in (1-cm) seam allowance, sew the two short ends together to form a tube. Zigzag the seam allowance.

5 Right sides together and taking a ⅜-in (1-cm) seam allowance, pin and then baste the circle of thick fabric into the bottom of the bag. Sew the seam, then zigzag stitch and trim, or serge, the seam allowance.

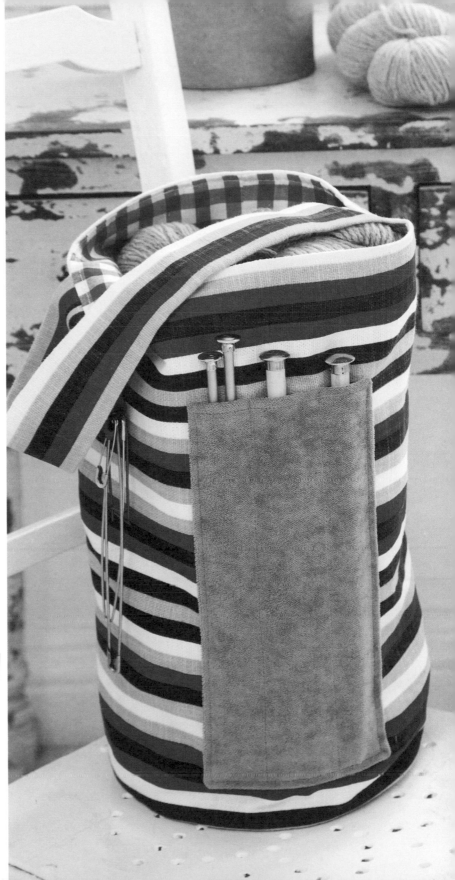

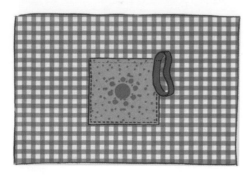

6 Make up the lining in the same way as the main bag. You can add as many pockets as you like to the inside of the bag. I like to have a loop of ribbon on to which I pin stitch holders, and a safety pin that I can find quickly if I drop a stitch. Leave a 4-in (10-cm) gap in the base seam for turning the bag through.

7 Right side in, fold the handle strip in half lengthwise and sew the seam, taking a ⅜-in (1-cm) seam allowance. Zigzag stitch and trim, or serge, the seam allowance. Turn the handle right side, roll the seam to center back, then press the handle flat.

8 Right sides together, pin the ends of the handle to the sides of the main bag, positioning them opposite one another and as you want in relation to the pocket position. Check that the handle isn't twisted. Set the sewing machine to a small zigzag stitch and sew across each end of the handle to attach it to the bag.

9 Right sides together (so the main bag is right side out and the lining is right side in), slip the main bag into the lining. Match the raw top edges of both pieces, making sure the handle is tucked down out of the way.

10 Sew around the top edges, taking a ⅜-in (1-cm) seam allowance. Zigzag stitch and trim, or serge, the seam allowance.

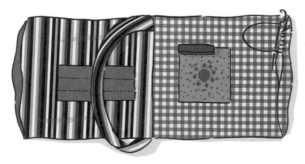

11 Gently pull the main bag right side out through the gap in the lining, then continue pulling until the lining is right-side out, too. Ladder stitch (see page 134) the gap in the lining closed. Tuck the lining back into the bag and you're done.

Patchwork

PINCUSHION

Another piece of sewing kit that's both cute and practical, this is a traditional pincushion design that looks perky in vintage or new fabrics. It's entirely hand-sewn, so makes an excellent lap project in front of a great movie on the television. (I won't try and recommend one in particular, but avoid anything with lovely men in small amounts of clothing, as distraction can lead to finger-stabbing with needles and pins.) And if you stuff the patchwork firmly and stop at Step 3, the resulting ball is a great baby toy.

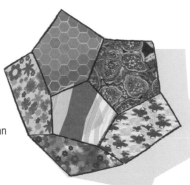

1 Using the pentagon templates (not the hexagon ones) and following Steps 1–8 of Hexie Cushion (see page 44), sew five pentagons to the edges of one central one. Because of the five-sided shape, the result will be a cup, rather than a flat patchwork. Make two the same.

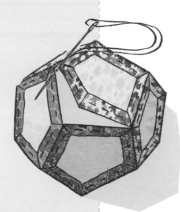

2 Fit the two cups together to make a ball, and sew them around the central seam, in the same way you sewed the pentagons together, leaving two edges open, as shown, but don't fasten off or cut the thread. Take out all the basting stitches and papers.

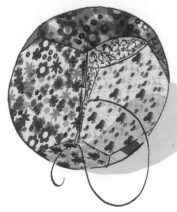

3 Turn the ball right side out, then fill it with toy stuffing. You need to stuff the ball fairly firmly for a pincushion —and firmer still if it's going to be a toy ball. Ladder stitch (see page 134) the gap closed and secure the thread.

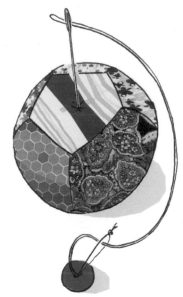

4 Thread the long needle with a long length of strong thread, double it, and knot the ends. From the back, take the needle through a hole in a button, then back through the other hole and between the threads above the knot. Pull tight, then push the needle straight down through the middle of the pincushion.

5 On the other side of the pincushion, thread on the second button. Take the needle back down through the other hole in it, and through the pincushion, then pull smoothly and firmly until the thread is as tight as possible and the buttons are deeply indented into the pincushion.

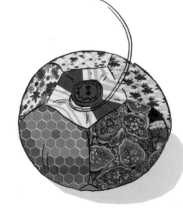

6 Wrap the thread around under the first button a couple of times to keep the tension, then stitch back and forth through the buttons and pincushion a few times. Secure the thread by wrapping and tying it under one of the buttons, then trim the ends.

Mirror,
MIRROR...

YOU'RE GOING TO NEED...
- For a bag with a finished size of 15¼ x 10¼in (38 x 26cm) and shoulder handles, two pieces of outer fabric each measuring 16 x 11in (40 x 28cm), two pieces of lining fabric each measuring 16 x 11in (40 x 28cm), one piece of pocket fabric measuring 11 x 7½in (28 x 19cm), and two pieces of handle fabric each measuring 22 x 5in (55 x 13cm)
- Fabric scissors
- Iron and ironing board
- Pins
- Sewing threads to match fabrics
- Sewing machine
- Hand-sewing needle
- Basting thread: I always use ordinary sewing thread in a contrast color
- 9in (23cm) zipper
- Fading fabric marker pen

Fabric totes have a zillion uses, are easy and quick to make, can be whatever size you need, can be decorated however you want, are a great way of using up leftover bits of fabric, make excellent gifts, are perfect for storing UFOs in a way that lets them be out of sight (thus avoiding too much guilt) but not so out of sight that you forget them entirely, are environment-friendly, can be made to match any outfit, and if you've made some of the previous projects in this book, then you've probably perfected most of the techniques needed. My bag has a plaid front and handles, a plain fabric back with plaid pocket, and a paisley design lining.

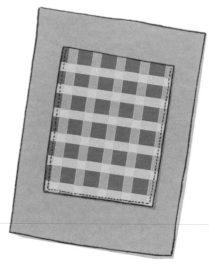

1 Follow Steps 1–2 of Knitter's Bucket Bag (see page 110) to make a pocket on one of the bag outer pieces. You can divide the pocket into smaller sections by following Step 3 as well, if you want to.

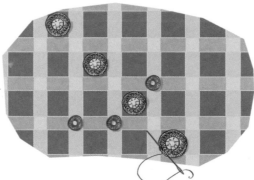

2 If you want to, decorate the other outer piece of the bag. I've used a selection of shisha mirrors and sequinned jewels, and sewed them on by hand.

3 Follow Step 7 of Knitter's Bucket Bag (see page 112) to make the two long strips of fabric into handles. Seam uppermost, pin and then zigzag stitch a handle to the top edge of the front and back bag pieces. Make sure that the handles aren't twisted before you sew them on.

NO ZIPPER
If you don't want the bag to be zipped, work Steps 1–4. Then sew the two bag outer pieces right sides together and turn the outer right side out. Sew the two lining pieces right sides together and leave them that way. Then follow Steps 9–11 of Knitter's Bucket Bag (see page 112) to make up the bag.

4 Now, follow Steps 10–17 of Yo-yo-a-go-go (see pages 53–54) to make up the bag. Just treat the handles as part of the bag outer and ignore them other than to make sure they don't get caught in any stitching. Make sure that the gap in the lining is in the middle of one side seam, not in the bottom seam.

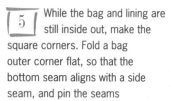

5 While the bag and lining are still inside out, make the square corners. Fold a bag outer corner flat, so that the bottom seam aligns with a side seam, and pin the seams together through all the layers. Measure down the seam 2in (5cm) from the point, and draw a line across the corner, at right angles to the seam, as shown. Machine-sew along this line, reversing at both ends to secure the stitching. Sew the other corner the same way, making sure that the seam allowance is lying to the same side.

6 Fold each corner over toward the bottom of the bag at the sewn line and hand-sew the point to the seam allowance of the bottom seam. Repeat Steps 5 and 6 on the corners of the lining. Then follow Step 18 of Yo-yo-a-go-go (see page 54) to finish the bag.

Angel STITCHING

YOU'RE GOING TO NEED...

- Cover and pages templates on page 140
- Paper for template
- Paper and fabric scissors
- Two pieces of felt for the cover and one piece for the pages, each measuring 5¼ x 4¾in (13 x 12cm)
- Piece of fusible webbing measuring 5¼ x 4¾in (13 x 12cm)
- Iron and ironing board
- Pencil
- Silver embroidery thread
- Embroidery needle
- Pins
- Sewing threads to match fabrics
- Tiny sew-on diamanté
- Towel

Like many sewing geeks, I adore kit that is both lovely looking and practical. If I had to choose between the two attributes, I hope I'd go for practical, but, honestly, it would depend on how lovely the useless thing was... Fortunately, this needlecase precludes the need to choose, and it's quick and simple to make: perfect! Filled with a selection of sharp needles and some lovely shiny pins, it is a perfect gift for any sewist.

1 Copy the cover template and cut it out. Fold the paper in half and lay the straight edge of the template on the fold. Draw around it and cut it out, then open it up to make a spread wings template. Do the same with the pages template.

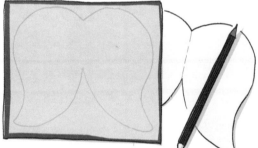

2 Iron the fusible webbing onto the back of one of the cover pieces of felt. Lay the cover template on the paper backing and draw around it with the pencil.

3 Cut out the cover. In pencil on the paper backing, draw simple curlicues onto the wings, branching out from the center, using the illustration as a guide. My wings aren't symmetrical, but that's just personal taste; I'm seriously not a fan of symmetry.

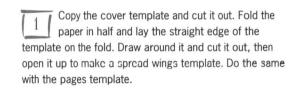

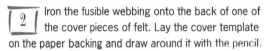

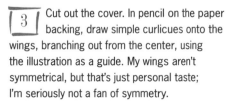

ANGEL STITCHING 119

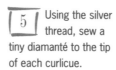

4 Using silver embroidery thread and chain stitch (see page 134), embroider the curlicues, checking that you are more-or-less following your drawn lines (doesn't have to be exact, the lines are there for guidance only) by turning the wings back and forth.

5 Using the silver thread, sew a tiny diamanté to the tip of each curlicue.

6 Lay the cover right side down on a towel (to cushion the diamanté) and peel off the paper backing: peel carefully to avoid pulling on the stitches too much. Lay the other piece of cover felt wrong side down on top of it and iron them together. Turn the cover right side up and cut around the embroidered front to cut out the completed cover.

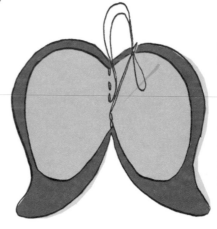

7 Using the pages template, cut out a page from the remaining piece of felt. (You can have more than one page, but beware your needlecase becoming too bulky to close.) Using doubled thread and continuous running stitch (see page 135), sew the page into the center of the cover.

8 Fold the needlecase in half and, using the towel to cushion the diamanté, press it firmly to set the central crease.

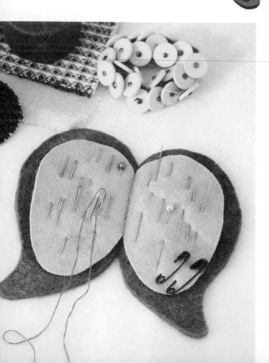

Roll up, ROLL UP

ROLL UP

YOU'RE GOING TO NEED...

- One piece of medium-weight main fabric measuring 16 x 18½in (40 x 47cm), for the back and one piece measuring 16 x 10¾in (40 x 27cm), for the front: I used needlecord
- One piece of lightweight contrast fabric measuring 16 x 10in (40 x 25cm): I used cotton
- Iron and ironing board
- Pins
- Sewing threads to match fabrics
- Sewing machine
- Fabric scissors
- Rotary cutter with pinking blade and cutting mat, or pinking shears
- Masking tape, or fading fabric marker, or quilting guide
- Strong sewing thread to match main fabric: I used topstitching thread
- Hand-sewing needle
- Button with a shank
- Cord long enough to wrap around the rolled-up roll a few times: I used 23½in (60cm) of leather

HOW MUCH FABRIC?

I've given the fabric sizes for this roll, which measures 15in (38cm) long when rolled out flat and holds needles up to 12in (30cm) long, but you can adjust sizes to suit your needle collection.

If, like most knitters, you cannot resist nice-looking knitting needles and have ended up with a needle stash that rivals your yarn stash, then a bespoke roll is what you need to keep everything organized and findable. A huge roll is a bit unwieldy, so if you do have lots of needles then do as I do, and make several rolls. You can store needles by sizes, materials (my preferred system), colors… whatever works for you.

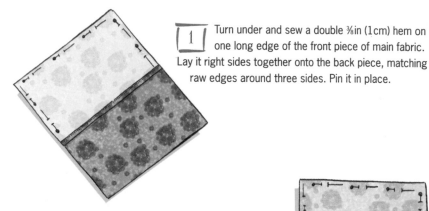

1 Turn under and sew a double ⅜in (1cm) hem on one long edge of the front piece of main fabric. Lay it right sides together onto the back piece, matching raw edges around three sides. Pin it in place.

2 Lay the contrast piece right sides together on the exposed half of the back piece, so that one edge overlaps the hemmed edge of the front, as shown. (To reduce bulk I used the selvage for this edge, or you can overcast or serge the edge to finish it.) Pin the layers together all around the edges.

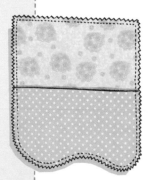

3 Taking a ⅜-in (1-cm) seam allowance, sew all around the edges. I sewed a wavy edge across what will be the flap, sewing the shape freehand; you can draw a shape onto the fabric first, or leave the flap edge straight if you prefer. Pink the seam allowance to finish it and reduce bulk. Clip the corners.

I LIKE TO MAKE...

4 Turn the roll right sides out through the overlapped edges and smooth the selvage/neatened edge of the contrast fabric flat under the hemmed edge. (This might sound a bit mysterious if you are just reading through, but when you come to do this it will make sense.) Keeping the hemmed edge rolled back out of the way, pin the selvage/neatened edge in place and machine-sew a straight line across the edge to hold it flat. You won't be able to get right to the ends, but that doesn't matter; just sew as far as you can.

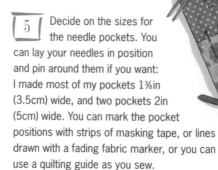

5 Decide on the sizes for the needle pockets. You can lay your needles in position and pin around them if you want: I made most of my pockets 1⅜in (3.5cm) wide, and two pockets 2in (5cm) wide. You can mark the pocket positions with strips of masking tape, or lines drawn with a fading fabric marker, or you can use a quilting guide as you sew.

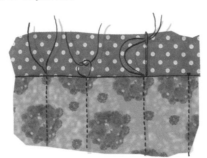

6 Using strong sewing thread, sew along the pocket lines, leaving long tails of thread at the start and finish of each line. Strengthen the pockets and secure the threads by knotting each pair of tails firmly, then threading them into the eye of a sewing needle and taking them into the hem (at the top) or the seam allowance (at the bottom).

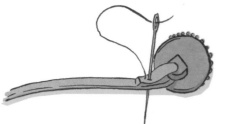

7 Thread one end of the cord through the button shank and sew it firmly in place.

8 Sewing through the shank, sew the button to one edge of the back of the roll, about halfway up the pockets, with the cord lying across the roll. Roll up the needle roll from the opposite end, then wrap the cord around the roll and secure it by wrapping it around the button a few times.

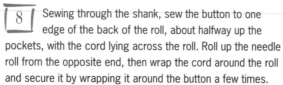

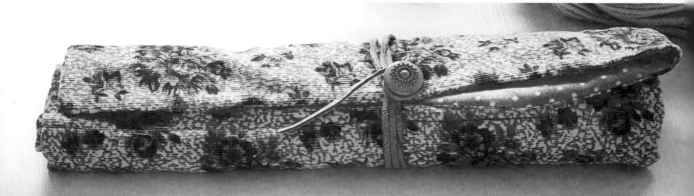

Pin SHARP

YOU'RE GOING TO NEED...

- 2in (5cm) of craft wire
- Thimble
- Epoxy glue
- 1½-in (4-cm) diameter circle of velvet
- Strong sewing thread
- Hand-sewing needle
- Polyester stuffing
- Ribbon for necklace: I used ¼-in (6-mm) wide velvet ribbon

WHAT KIND OF FABRIC?

Velvet is good because it doesn't show pin marks, but if the pincushion is going to be jewelry only, then you can use any fabric that isn't thick or stiff. I have found that a 4in (10cm) circle is about right for an average-size thimble.

Out yourself as a sewist with a necklace that's useful as well as cute. ("Useful?" I hear you say: these pincushions are great when you are pinning for fit on a dress form or friend.) And it's super-easy, quick, and thrifty to make, and a great way of putting widely available and sweet sewing lovelies to good use, and the best gift for sewist friends. What more could you want?

1 | Bend and twist the wire to form a loop with a twisted neck and curly feet, as shown.

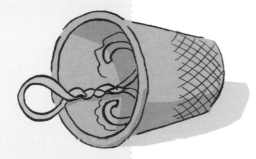

2 | Press the curly feet inside the thimble so that they bend to fit against the side, then set the loop aside. Mix up a dollop of epoxy glue (follow the packet instructions) and put it in the thimble against what will be the back side. Press the curly feet into the glue, so that just the loop protrudes above the rim of the thimble, and let dry.

3 Using doubled strong sewing thread, work a line of small running stitches around the edge of the velvet circle.

4 Put a ball of stuffing in the center of the circle and pull the gathers up around it. Add more stuffing if need be to make the pincushion as firm as you want it (I like mine to be really quite firm indeed).

HUNT THE THIMBLE
One thing you have to remember when looking for a thimble to make this pincushion is that any decoration needs to work when the thimble is, in effect, upside down. Lots of thimbles have motifs that are the right way up when the thimble is on your finger; so something like a bird can look very odd (and very dead) lying on its back, feet in the air, around your neck.

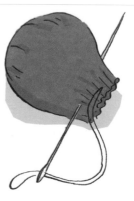

5 Pull the gathers up as tight as possible and stitch back and forth through them to secure them. Cut the thread short.

6 | Mix up a little more epoxy glue and spread it inside the thimble. Press the stuffed velvet ball down into the thimble, as shown, and let dry. Loop the ribbon through the wire loop and tie the ends to make a necklace the length you prefer.

Vacation
STITCHES

YOU'RE GOING TO NEED...

- One piece of medium-weight fabric measuring 13¾ x 12½in (35 x 31cm), one piece measuring 13¾ x 10¾in (35 x 27cm), and one piece measuring 13¾ x 2½in (35 x 6cm): I used needlecord
- 10in (25cm) zipper
- Piece of very heavy fusible interfacing measuring 13 x 5⅝in (33 x 14cm): I used shirt canvas
- Fabric scissors
- Hand-sewing needle
- Basting thread: I always use ordinary sewing thread in a contrast color
- Iron and ironing board
- Pins
- Sewing threads to match fabrics
- Sewing machine
- Piece of strong felt measuring 4 x 5½in (10 x 14cm) for the scissor holder, and a scrap for the tab
- Snap fastener
- Decorative button
- Piece of thinner felt measuring 3 x 4¾in (8 x 12cm) for the needle and pin holder
- 31in (80cm) of ⅜-in (1-cm) wide grosgrain ribbon
- Piece of fusible webbing measuring 12½ x 4¾in (31 x 12cm)
- Masking tape

A vacation isn't a vacation without something to do. Not something work related! Something lovely to sew is what's needed. And for that you need some kit. And to hold the kit you need a little caddy of some kind. One like this, maybe? It has safe storage for your scissors, needles, and pins, and a pocket for other bits and bobs. This version holds a pair of dressmaking scissors 8¼in (21cm) long, but you can easily adjust the sizes of the pieces to hold larger shears, or make a smaller caddy that holds embroidery scissors.

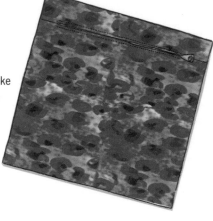

1 Follow Steps 2–5 of Wrap Up Warm (see pages 74–75) to make the two smaller pieces of fabric and the zipper into a pocket piece.

2 Lay the pocket piece right side down and flat and position the piece of heavy interfacing at the bottom, as shown, ⅜in (1cm) in from the raw edges. Iron it in place.

3 Cut the piece of strong felt into a blunt-tipped triangle that will accommodate your scissors.

I LIKE TO MAKE...

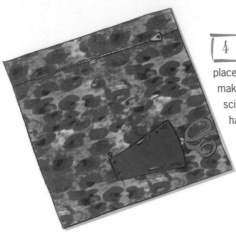

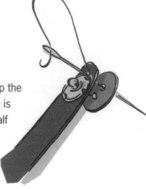

4 | Position the scissor holder on the right side of the pocket piece, on the interfaced section, and pin in place. You might need to push the top edges in a bit to make the pocket three-dimensional so that it holds the scissors comfortably. Then machine-sew (like me) or hand-sew the pocket in place.

5 | Cut a strip of felt to make a tab to stop the scissors falling out of the holder; mine is 2½in (6cm) long and ⅝in (1.5cm) wide. Sew half a snap fastener to the wrong side of one end and a decorative button to the other side of the same end.

6 | With the scissors in the holder, pin the tab and other half of the snap fastener in place so that when the tab is fastened, it loops over one handle of the scissors. Sew the pieces in position.

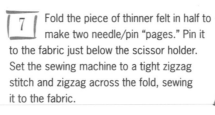

7 | Fold the piece of thinner felt in half to make two needle/pin "pages." Pin it to the fabric just below the scissor holder. Set the sewing machine to a tight zigzag stitch and zigzag across the fold, sewing it to the fabric.

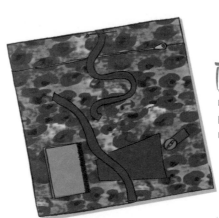

8 | Cut the ribbon in half and baste one end to the middle of each long edge of the pocket piece, so that the cut end matches the edge of the fabric.

I LIKE TO MAKE...

9 Lay the pocket piece face down. Center the fusible webbing on the interfacing and iron it in place.

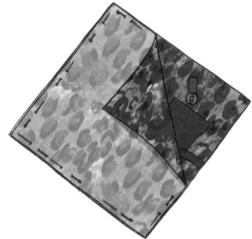

10 Open the zipper halfway: this is essential. Right sides together, lay the largest piece of fabric over the pocket piece, matching the edges. Pin the layers together around the edges, making sure the ribbons are tucked out of the way. Taking a ⅜-in (1-cm) seam allowance, sew right around the edges. Clip the corners off the seam allowances. Peel the paper backing off the fusible webbing.

11 Turn the caddy right side out through the open zipper, pushing out the corners neatly. Make sure that the layers are flat and smooth, then iron the back of the interfaced section to bond the layers together with the fusible webbing.

12 On the front, mark the edge of the interfaced section with a strip of masking tape (you'll be able to feel the edge of the interfacing through the fabric). Sew along the edge of the tape to form the bottom edge of the pocket.

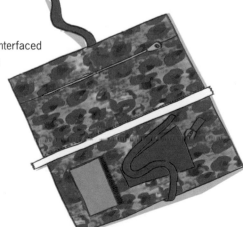

Techniques

TRANSFERRING DESIGNS ONTO FABRIC

On pages 138–143 are the templates for some of the projects in this book, and you'll need to transfer them on to fabric if you want to copy a project exactly.

If you only need the outline of a shape, then just enlarge the template to the right size on a photocopier (all the templates give the correct enlargement percentage), and cut it out. Pin it to the fabric. If you're used to cutting out patterns, or it's a fairly simple shape, just cut out around the edges of the template. Otherwise, draw around it with a fading fabric marker pen (don't be tempted to use an ordinary pen or pencil, as they can permanently mark and spoil your project), then remove the template and cut out the shape. If there are marks within the template that you need, then follow Steps 1–3 of Tattooed Lady (see page 13) to transfer them on to the fabric.

CLIPPING CURVED SEAM ALLOWANCES

This helps curved seams lie flat and will make a real difference to the look of your finished project.

Use the tips of your fabric scissors (don't use tiny embroidery scissors as this will dull the blades) to cut into the seam allowance after stitching, taking great care not to cut through any of the stitches. Seams that curve outward need wedge-shaped notches cut into the seam allowance, while for seams that will curve inward, little slits will do (though I usually just cut notches in both types of seam).

TRIMMING CORNERS

For corners, you need to snip off the excess fabric across the point before you turn the project right side out, so that the finished corner is neat and square. Cut off the fabric across the corner about ⅛in (3mm) away from the stitching, taking care not to cut through the stitches.

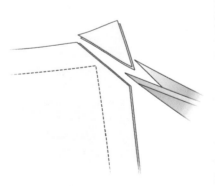

STITCHES

These are the embroidery and utility hand stitches used in the projects.

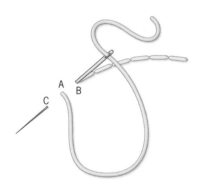

Backstitch

Before the sewing machine was invented, this is what you used to sew up seams. And it's a versatile embroidery stitch.

Working from right to left, bring the needle up at A, down at B, and up at C, one stitch length ahead of A. For the next stitch, go down at A and come up a stitch length ahead of C, and continue along in this way.

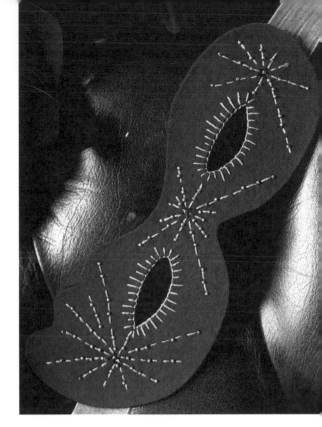

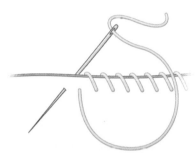

Whip stitch

This is used to join fabrics either right sides or wrong sides together.

Hold together the two pieces of fabric, matching the edges to be joined. From the back, take the needle through both pieces, close to the edge. Take the needle over the edges and to the back and through both pieces again a short distance further along, pulling the thread taut to complete the stitch. If you are joining the fabrics wrong sides together, you can hide the starting knot between the layers.

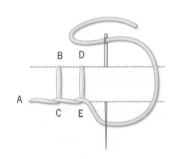

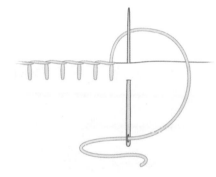

Blanket stitch

Another stitch that's both utility and decorative. Use it to sew one piece of fabric to another, or just as an embroidery stitch, or work it along an edge, or use it to join two edges.

Bring the needle up at A, down at B, and up at C (directly below B), looping the thread under the tip of the needle. Pull the needle through, then insert it at D and bring it out at E, again looping the thread under the tip.

If you are working it along an edge, the principle is the same, but the horizontal bar of thread lies along the edge of the fabric, as shown.

Chain stitch

This is a marvellous stitch—easy to work, forgiving of inexperience, and very good-looking.

Bring the needle up at A, then insert it at the same point. Make a short stitch to B, looping the thread under the tip of the needle.

Pull the thread through to form the first loop in the chain. Insert the needle at B again and make another short stitch to C (the same length as the A to B stitch), then loop the thread under the tip of the needle. Continue, keeping all the stitches the same length. To anchor the last stitch in the chain, take the needle down just outside the loop, forming a little bar over it.

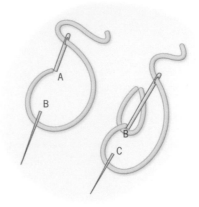

Fly stitch

As well as being great for stitching down buttons decoratively (see page 53), fly stitch is also a lovely embroidery stitch.

Bring the needle up at A and down at B, leaving a loop of thread. Bring the needle up inside the loop at C and pull the loop taut, then take the needle down at D, outside the loop. The C to D stitch can be long or short, as you prefer.

French knot

Practice these stitches on a leftover piece of the project fabric to get the tension right.

Bring the needle up at A, wrap the thread tightly around it twice, then insert the needle very close to A. Hold the wraps down with the thumbnail of your non-sewing hand, and pull the needle and working thread slowly and carefully through the wraps and fabric to form a small knot.

Ladder stitch

This is the best stitch for closing up the gap in a machine- or hand-sewn seam once the project has been turned right side out.

Turn in the seam allowances across the gap and press them (with your fingers or an iron). Bring the needle up through the pressed fold at A, then take it straight across the gap to B. Make a tiny stitch through the folded edge and bring it back to the front at C. Continue in this way, zigzagging from one side to another and making the stitches equally spaced.

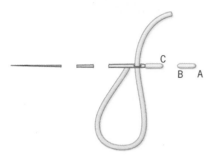

Running stitch

Another multi-purpose stitch: use it for basting (not worrying about stitch length or tidiness), for decoration, or for gathering.

Bring the needle up at A, down at B, and up at C, and continue in this way. If being used decoratively, you can space the stitches evenly and make them all the same length, or work them more randomly, depending on the look you want.

Continuous running stitch

This is a useful stitch that forms a solid line of stitching, but unlike backstitch (see page 133), it looks the same on both sides.

Work a line of running stitch (see left), then work back along the line, filling in the gaps with a second line of running stitch.

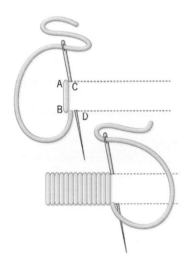

Satin stitch

The secret of success with this stitch is getting the tension right. You can outline the shape to be satin stitched with split stitch (see right), which gives a defined edge that's easier to keep neat than if you just follow a drawn outline.

Bring the needle up at A, down at B, up at C, down at D, and so on, working the stitches close together so that no fabric shows in between them.

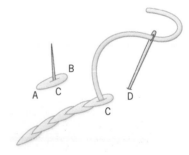

Split stitch

This is used to outline shapes to be satin stitched (see left), but it's also an embroidery stitch in its own right; it looks a bit like miniature chain stitch (see page 134).

Make a short stitch from A to B. Bring the needle up at C, halfway along the stitch and splitting the thread. Continue in this way, making the stitches all the same length and splitting them at the same point along that length.

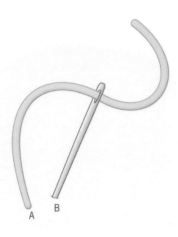

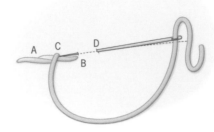

Stab stitch

Yet another stitch that's both utility and decorative.

Simply bring the needle up at A and take it down at B, making a short, straight stitch.

Stem stitch

My favorite outlining stitch, this is a quick and easy stitch to work. Note that it's worked from left to right.

Bring the needle up at A and down at B. Bring it back up at C, halfway between A and B, making sure the thread is below or to the right of the needle (depending on the direction you are working in). Take the needle down at D and bring it out at B, at the end of the last stitch.

Work outline stitch in the same way, but have the thread above or to the left of the needle as you work.

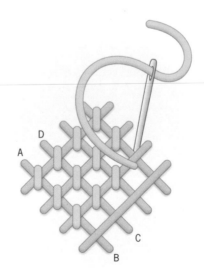

Trellis stitch

This is a great filler stitch that covers an area quickly. It can be worked at any angle.

Make a series of long straight stitches; A to B, then C to D, and so on to cover the area. Then make more stitches in the same way at right angles to the first set. If the stitches are long then hold them down at the intersections with tiny stab stitches (see above left).

CROCHET

Granny squares

If you want to include granny squares in the Do Away with Damp project on page 58, then this is the pattern I used. I chose a worsted-weight (Aran) yarn and used a G/6 (4.5mm) crochet hook. Note that the pattern is worked using American terminology; see the list of abbreviations below for UK equivalents.

Ch 6. Join with a sl st to form a ring.
Round 1: Ch 3, this counts as the first dc. Work 2 more dc into ring, [ch 3, 3 dc into ring] 3 times. Ch 3, sl st to join to beginning of round. *12 dc*
Join a new color to any ch-3 space using a sl st.
Round 2: Ch 3, this counts as the first dc. 2 dc, ch 3, 3 dc into same space, ch 1 [3 dc, ch 3, 3 dc in next 3-ch space, ch 1] 3 times. Sl st to join to beginning of round. *24 dc*
Join a new color to any ch-3 space using a sl st.
Round 3: Ch 3, this counts as the first dc. 2 dc, ch 3, 3 dc into same space, ch 1 [3 dc, ch 3, 3 dc in next 1-ch space, ch 1, 3 dc, ch 3, 3 dc in next 3-ch space] 3 times. Sl st to join to beginning of round. *36 dc*
Continue in the same way—working 3 dc into every 1-ch space in the previous round, and two lots of 3 dc separated by 3 ch into each corner space—until the square is as large as you want it to be.
Work one round of sc all around the finished square: this will act as the seam allowance.

Crochet abbreviations

US		UK	
dc	double crochet	tr	treble crochet
sc	single crochet	dc	double crochet
sl st	slip stitch	ss	slip stitch

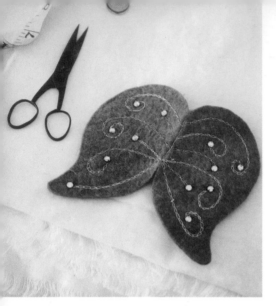

Templates

This section contains all the templates you will need. Where a template is not given at actual size, simply photocopy it at the percentage indicated in order to enlarge it.

BUTTON-ON BROOCH

(page 104)

ACTUAL SIZE

YO-YO-A-GO-GO

(page 50)

QUARTER-SIZE TEMPLATE:

photocopy by 400%

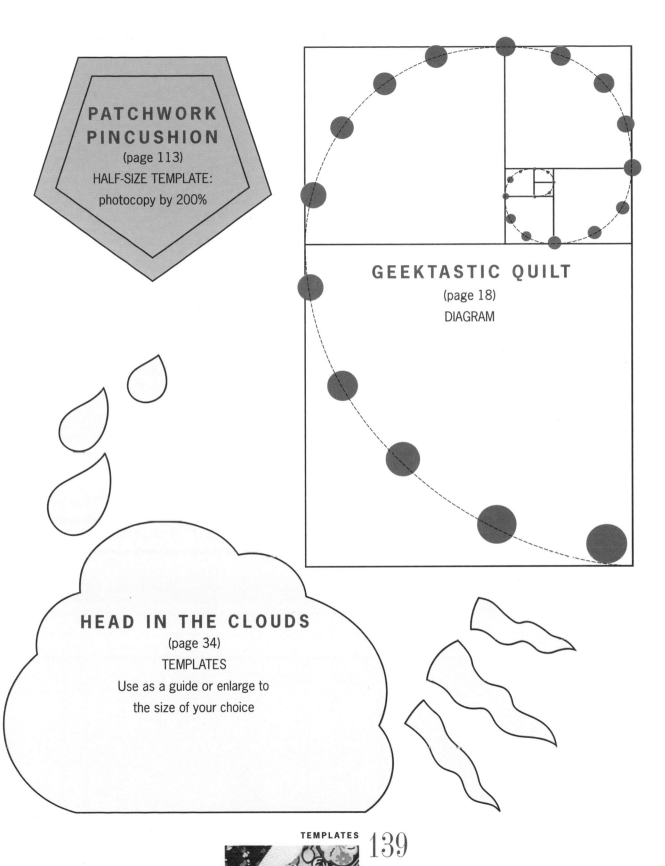

PATCHWORK
PINCUSHION
(page 113)
HALF-SIZE TEMPLATE:
photocopy by 200%

GEEKTASTIC QUILT
(page 18)
DIAGRAM

HEAD IN THE CLOUDS
(page 34)
TEMPLATES
Use as a guide or enlarge to
the size of your choice

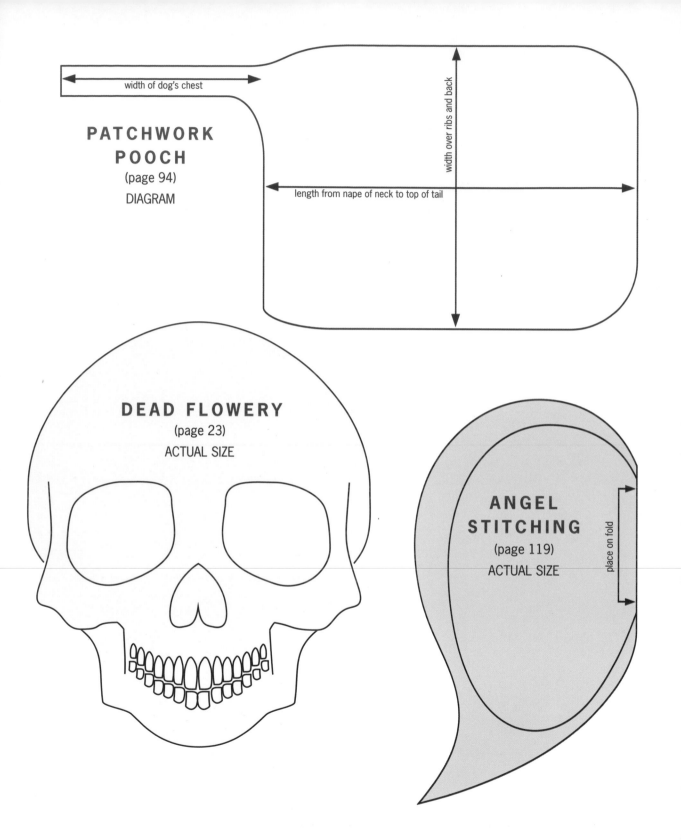

PATCHWORK POOCH
(page 94)
DIAGRAM

width of dog's chest

width over ribs and back

length from nape of neck to top of tail

DEAD FLOWERY
(page 23)
ACTUAL SIZE

ANGEL STITCHING
(page 119)
ACTUAL SIZE

place on fold

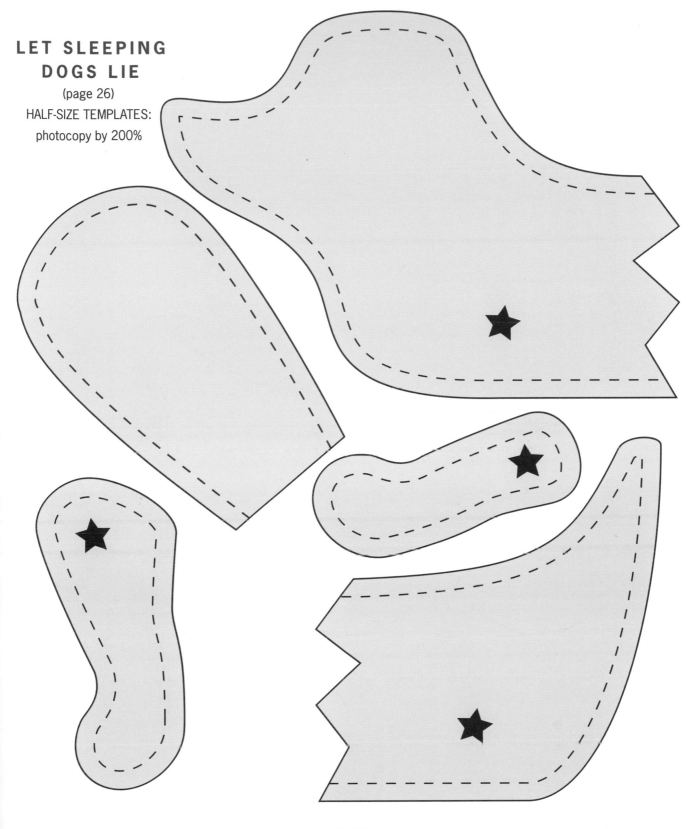

LET SLEEPING DOGS LIE

(page 26)
HALF-SIZE TEMPLATES:
photocopy by 200%

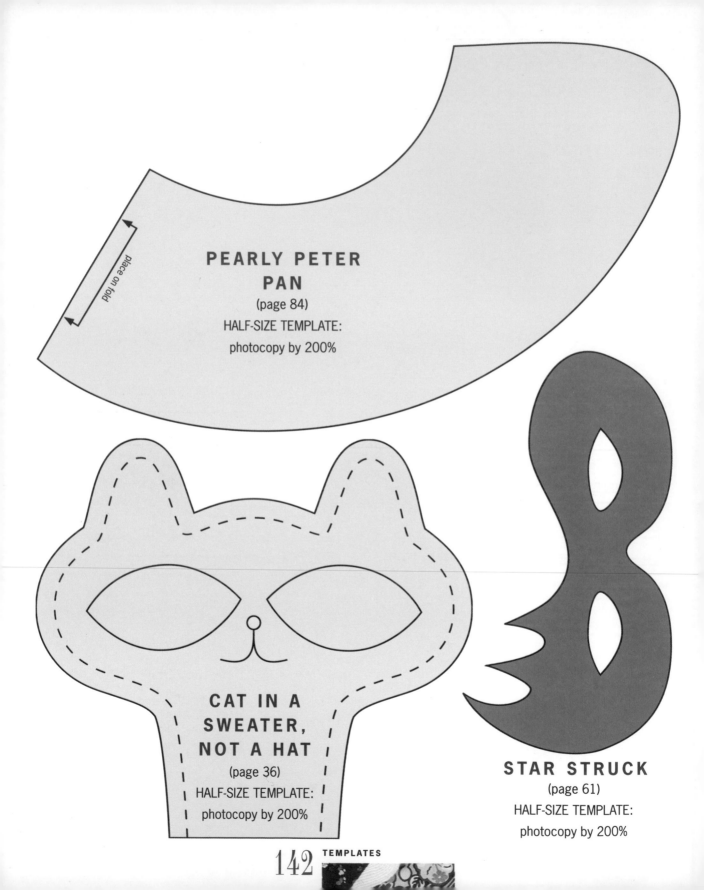

**PEARLY PETER
PAN**
(page 84)
HALF-SIZE TEMPLATE:
photocopy by 200%

place on fold

**CAT IN A
SWEATER,
NOT A HAT**
(page 36)
HALF-SIZE TEMPLATE:
photocopy by 200%

STAR STRUCK
(page 61)
HALF-SIZE TEMPLATE:
photocopy by 200%

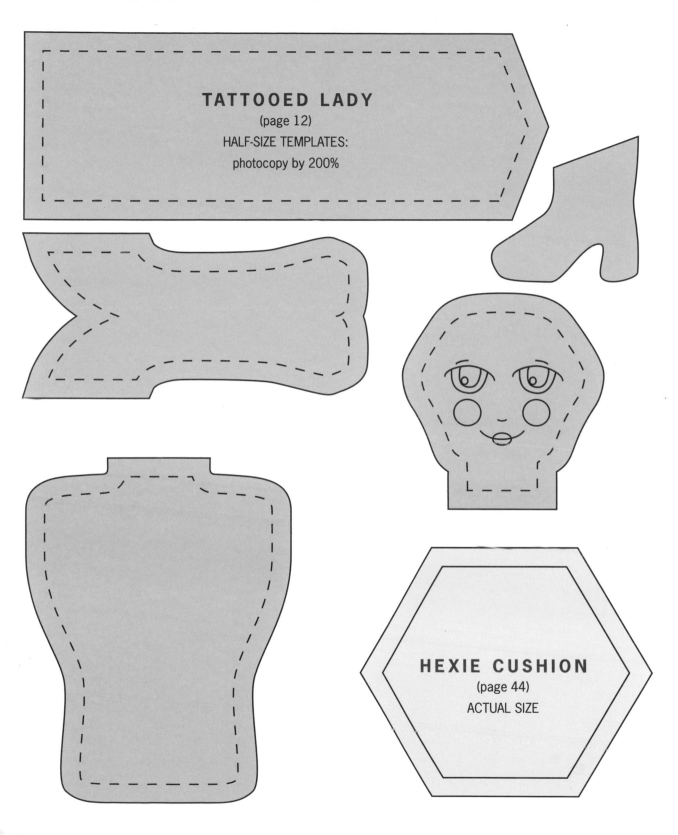

TATTOOED LADY

(page 12)

HALF-SIZE TEMPLATES:

photocopy by 200%

HEXIE CUSHION

(page 44)

ACTUAL SIZE

Index

Suppliers

US

Fabricland
www.fabricland.com
J&O Fabrics
www.jandofabrics.com
Jo-Ann Fabric and Craft Stores
www.joann.com
Michaels stores
www.michaels.com
Hobby Lobby
www.hobbylobby.com
Purl Soho
www.purlsoho.com

UK

The Eternal Maker
www.eternalmaker.com
Supplier of fabulous jumbo rick rack.
Guthrie & Ghani
www.guthrie-ghani.co.uk
Lovely fabrics and haberdashery, and lovely staff.
John Lewis
www.johnlewis.com
Great sewing equipment and some fabrics.
Liberty
www.liberty.com
Lovely sewing equipment, haberdashery, and fabrics.
Fabrics Galore
www.fabricsgalore.co.uk
Always my first stop on a fabric shop. Great range at excellent prices.
Creative Quilting
www.creativequilting.co.uk
Good range of fabrics and very helpful staff. Also sell some embroidery floss and sewing equipment.
The Cloth House
www.clothhouse.com
My favorite fabric shop, with a range of acrylic/wool mix felts.

Acknowledgments

My thanks to Cindy Richards at CICO for continuing to give me the opportunity to make books, and to Carmel Edmonds for keeping *Sewlicious* on track. Thank you to Katie Hardwicke for her efficient and accurate editorial work; to Sania Pell, Jo Henderson, Catherine Woram, and Penny Wincer for the lovely photographs and styling; to Michael Hill for his illustrations; and to Elizabeth Healey for making the pages look so good. Thanks, as ever, to Philip for the food.